BETTE HAGMAN

THE GLUTEN-FREE GOURMET

Living Well Without Wheat

HENRY HOLT AND COMPANY
NEW YORK

Henry Holt and Company, Inc.
Publishers since 1866
115 West 18th Street
New York, New York 10011

Henry Holt® is a registered trademark
of Henry Holt and Company, Inc.

Published in Canada by Fitzhenry & Whiteside Ltd.,
195 Allstate Parkway, Markham, Ontario L3R 4T8.

Library of Congress Cataloging-in-Publication Data
Hagman, Bette.
The gluten-free gourmet : living well without wheat /
by Bette Hagman.—1st ed.
p. cm.
Includes bibliographical references.
1. Gluten-free diet—Recipes.   I. Title.
RM237.9.H34   1990   89-20116
641.5'63—dc20   CIP

ISBN 0-8050-1210-9
ISBN 0-8050-1835-2 (An Owl Book : pbk.)

Henry Holt books are available for special promotions
and premiums. For details contact: Director, Special Markets.

First published in hardcover in 1990 by
Henry Holt and Company, Inc.

First Owl Book Edition—1991

Designed by Kate Nichols

Printed in the United States of America
All first editions are printed on acid-free paper.∞

5   7   9   10   8   6   4
7   9   11   13   15   14   12   10   8
pbk.

TO JOE AND DONNA JO,
MY TASTER AND MY TESTER

CONTENTS

PREFACE

The Gluten-free Gourmet is more than a collection of diet recipes. All the recipes in this book were developed and tested in my own kitchen after I was told by my doctor to eliminate wheat, oats, barley, and rye from my diet.

I didn't start out to write a book, but, like Topsy, it just grew from a file of my recipes typed to share with other celiacs and, to my surprise, friends who didn't need to avoid gluten but enjoyed the dishes.

As the file grew, I found I had nearly a bookful of tasty ideas to help others avoid the frustrations of watching their companions eat the wheat-laden bread, cake, cookies, and pasta forbidden on our diet. I knew the feeling; I had once suffered it, but now that I had developed recipes for all of these, I wanted to share them.

This collection does not include recipes for plain vegetables, meat, or fruit dishes that one can find in other cookbooks. I concentrated on the baked goods, mixed dishes, and pastas that we usually have to forgo. Although we should be wary of mixed salads when eating out because of the dressings—or the pasta or croutons that might be added—we can easily modify most salad recipes to make our own fruit or vegetable combinations.

Since my main concern was to create the best-tasting dishes I could devise using the tricky gluten-free flours, I made no special attempt to keep the recipes low in cholesterol, sodium free, low in calories or high in fiber. But since many celiacs, especially those recently diagnosed, have a problem with lactose, I tried, whenever possible, to give a choice of a nondairy substitute for a dairy product.

If you are lactose intolerant, you may delete the dry milk powder called for in the yeast bread recipes and substitute, instead, equal amounts of powdered baby formula: Isomil, ProSobee, Nursoy (soy-based), or Pregestimil (corn-based). Each formula reacts differently and the taste varies. If the bread dough feels too thin, add up to $1/2$ cup more rice flour in the first beating.

Many of these recipes may be further altered to fit other dietetic needs. The diabetic can replace the sugar with special sugar substitutes. For baking, the best product results when the substitute sugar is used in the heavier, moister cakes (for example, carrot cake, apple raisin cake, and the like). Those who cannot tolerate soy can replace the soy flour in a recipe with rice flour. (Since soy is more moist, use a bit more liquid.) They should also avoid nondairy substitutes, as most of them are soy based.

In some of the recipes, the amount of cholesterol may be lowered by changing the specified meats and cheeses to those with less cholesterol or by using egg substitutes in place of real eggs. Or you may substitute 2 egg whites for one whole egg; 3 egg whites for 2 eggs. The egg exchange works best in baking if the recipe calls for two eggs or less.

For those who are watching their sodium intake, herbs and spices, light salt, or salt substitute can replace some or all of the salt. Some of the cheeses may be exchanged for varieties lower in sodium.

For those who wish more fiber, it would be easy to substitute brown rice flour for the white in many of the recipes, to add rice bran in some, and to include more high-fiber vegetables in the casseroles and soups.

Many of the cakes, pies, and other desserts are, admittedly, high in calories, but no higher than similar desserts baked with regular flours. For those counting calories, my only suggestion is to serve smaller portions and, as I do, invite others to share so there will be no leftovers.

Whether you use the recipes as I have written them or alter them to fit other dietary needs, it is my hope that these recipes will make your cooking without gluten more tasty and a lot easier.

B.H.

ACKNOWLEDGMENTS

No cookbook is the work of a single person. Some of these recipes were created in my own kitchen, but for the rest I have many people to thank: other celiacs who so willingly shared their gluten-free recipes, interested friends who suggested revisions to their favorite dishes, and finally, the authors of the many cookbooks I browsed to get ideas: the Rombauer/Becker *Joy of Cooking*, *Better Homes and Gardens New Cookbook*, and, especially, Betty Wason and her *The Everything Cookbook*.

I owe a great debt to the specialists who reviewed the book while in progress and added valuable suggestions: Jan and Dr. Eugene Winkelman, Cleveland Clinic Foundation; Frances Tyus, R.D., L.D., of the Cleveland Clinic Foundation; Leon Rottman, President CSA/USA; Gladys Johnson, CSA/USA; and Judy Bodmer, R.D., formerly with Swedish Hospital, Seattle.

I also thank my family for their patience, my friends for their honesty, my celiac testers for their ideas, and my writing group for critiquing this cookbook when they would have much preferred to hear the Great American Novel. Last, I'm indebted to Elaine I. Hartsook, Ph.D., R.D., founder of the Gluten Intolerance Group of North America, for her years of support and information.

Grateful acknowledgment is made to Margaret Powers Nance for the sourdough rice bread recipe (Celiac Sourdough Bread) from her book *Gluten Free and Good!* (Oldtown Press, Kentucky, 1983), copyright © 1983 by Margaret Powers; to Judy Lew for the Chinese Corn Soup recipe from her book *Enjoy Chinese Cuisine* (Joie, Inc., Tokyo, Japan, 1984), copyright © 1984 by Judy Lew; and to Pat Murphy Garst for her recipe for pizza crust (Pat's Thin Yeast Crust).

FOREWORD

"If the patient can be cured at all, it must be by means of diet." Not a surprising statement when it is recognized that dietary management was the primary and often sole treatment of gastrointestinal disorders 110 years ago; however, the author, Samuel Gee, an English physician, also specified that "the allowance of farinaceous (starchy) foods must be small." His treatise "On the Coeliac Affection," published in 1888, described and discussed sprue in such an incisive, accurate manner that the article became a classic example of medical writing. Unfortunately, another century passed before clinical observation and application of the developing scientific method eventually produced the answer to the myriad ills of celiac disease, idiopathic steatorrhea, nontropical sprue, adult celiac disease, gluten-induced enteropathy, all of which are now regarded as synonymous with celiac sprue.

Starches, other carbohydrates, and fats were the foods invariably excluded from the diets of celiac patients, but starch remained the prime suspect. The "banana diet," introduced in 1924, then became the diet of choice, particularly for the pediatric age group, but this slowly vanished from the treatment manual after 1950 when the doctoral thesis of W. K. Dicke, a Dutch doctor, demonstrated that remission of the disorder could be obtained by "eliminating certain types of flour, especially wheat and rye flour" from the diet. During World War II, Dicke had observed that children with celiac disease improved and the number of new cases decreased considerably. The correlation between this change in the disease pattern and the scarcity of cereal grains in wartime Holland, and the return of celiac disease to its prewar prominence when grain once again became readily available, led to his investigations. Chemically, wheat flour consists primarily of starch and water, and to a lesser degree protein and a very minimal amount of fat. The starch and protein can be separated, and when these are analyzed, gluten is found only within the protein portion. From the gluten, which makes up 90 percent of the protein, a much smaller amount of a second protein, gliadin, can be isolated. It is in this fraction of the gluten that the toxic activity resides. Hence, after almost a hundred years of incrimination, starch has been absolved of complicity in this disorder and the actual culprit identified.

Over the next ten years, Dr. Dicke, his collaborators, and many other investigators recorded the success of the gluten-free diet in alleviating the symptoms of celiac sprue, while at the same time other researchers demonstrated the toxic effect of gluten and gliadin on the absorptive surface of the small intestine. Unfortunately, there were a few individuals who did not respond to this diet, and thus it was not until the 1960s that the gluten-free diet was accepted by the medical community as standard treatment. Prior to that time, the efficacy of adrenocortical hormones in promoting rapid improvement in the sprue patient had provided an acceptable alternative therapy, but at present there is no need for the use of this medication except for the occasional individual who does not respond to the elimination of gluten.

Failure to respond to the prescribed gluten-free diet is almost invariably due to an inability to maintain the diet, either because of lack of commitment on the part of the patient and the patient's family or the inability to ferret out the presence of wheat flour, which is pervasive in the diet of the average American family. Less frequent problems occur in the occasional individual who reacts to other foodstuffs, such as milk or eggs, or who has a different absorptive or other underlying medical problem. Medical dogma states that if the patient does not respond to the program within a month or so, the diet must be reviewed and, if necessary, the patient hospitalized in order to eat food prepared and served under the supervision of an experienced dietetic department. Patients do vary in their sensitivity to gluten, and whereas some can tolerate sizable amounts, others may be exquisitely sensitive to it. Since the definition of sprue implicitly requires a response to the withdrawal of gluten, the failure to become asymptomatic implies not only a failure to completely eliminate gluten from the diet, but also the possibility of an erroneous diagnosis, a complication, or the very unusual instance where the patient is refractory.

One of the most rewarding experiences in a physician's career is diagnosing celiac sprue. In a moment, the doctor has not only named but has also explained the reason for the varied mysterious ills that may have been present anywhere from weeks to a lifetime. Suddenly, the patient hears that this bizarre disorder with the totally strange name is a curable disease. However, elation at the knowledge that the patient need no longer be considered a hypochondriac is rapidly tempered by the doctor's warning that from here on life must be lived without wheat, rye, barley, and oats. Patients quickly realize that a certain paranoia about their foodstuffs is a necessity and that not only must they read the fine print on labels, they must also be prepared to challenge it. Exposure to gluten, with the subsequent return of symptoms, lurks in unexpected places. Bette Hagman's chapter on the hidden glutens describes the many pitfalls that await the celiac. Another example of many unrecognized hazards is a patient whose disease was considered refractory until it was discovered that wheat flour was used to separate the films that he sorted at work. Once he was transferred to another area free of flour, his symptoms disappeared while he continued on the same strict diet that he had followed previously. The section on traveling and dining out is an excellent primer that provides the means to avoid both embarrassment and trouble when away from one's own table.

But most important of all is the stress placed on the need to accept the fact that maintenance of the gluten-free diet must be a lifelong obligation, no matter how quickly one responds to the diet or how well one feels. There can be no dispute that life as a celiac is difficult, especially for the child and young adult to whom peer pressure and the need to conform can be most important aspects of everyday life. Adherence to the diet is particularly vital in this group, because in their growing years they are particularly vulnerable to the loss of those nutrients necessary for them to achieve their complete physical and mental promise. A feeling of wellness breeds a sense of complacency, and it becomes an easy matter to slip out of a long-established pattern with a recurrence of symptoms that may be so subtle as to escape early recognition.

Mrs. Hagman has shared her insights and her resources; this is a splendid text. Although it is an impossible task to answer every question in regard to understanding and complying with the gluten-free diet, she has accomplished what she set out to do by compiling not only a cookbook but truly "a diet for life and a prescription for living."

Eugene Winkelman, M.D., F.A.C.P.
Cleveland Clinic Foundation
Cleveland, Ohio

The Gluten-free Gourmet

A Diet for Life

When I left my doctor's office fifteen years ago clutching three smudged photocopied pages, I was sure that he, like all the other physicians over the years, was just trying to mollify one more skinny hypochondriac. How could a simple diet relieve me of years of bloating, gas, pain, and bouts of diarrhea? I had never heard of nontropical sprue, the term he gave my disease.

One week later, I called his office. "You're a genius. I feel better already."

"Just stick to that gluten-free diet and call me back when you start gaining some weight."

By the end of the month, I'd read everything I could find (and that wasn't much) about my condition, which had several names: nontropical sprue, celiac sprue, gluten enteropathy and, finally, celiac disease. The symptoms were familiar. Another gluten-intolerant condition, dermatitis herpetiformis, had symptoms of burning blisters, bumps, or lesions. I also discovered that I was fortunate in having been diagnosed in the 1970s. Although physicians were aware of celiac disease long before that, until the 1950s, there was no answer to what caused the distress symptoms. Many sufferers were limited to eating bananas and rice and were forbidden coarse foods like vegetables, meat, and other fruits. It wasn't until after World War II that diets could be expanded, when doctors became aware that only the gluten in wheat, oats, barley, and rye was intolerable to patients with celiac sprue.

I also discovered, though, that with my improved health and renewed appetite, a diet without wheat, oats, barley, or rye was just plain boring. I didn't mind Cream of Rice for breakfast, but how could I live the rest of my life without bread or pasta or cake or stuffing in my turkey or . . . ? The list became endless. One day I cheated and ate some freshly baked bread full of the forbidden glutens.

The result of that spree was three days in bed suffering the same distress that had sent me to the doctor. I didn't tell him about my slip, but I resolved it would never happen again. Until medical science came up with a medicine to cure our disease, I'd stick to my diet. I also pledged myself to finding some way to make my food more interesting.

Since I am the kind of noncook who left the plastic wrap on the corned beef the first time I tried boiling it, and who had to look up the word *sauté* in the dictionary, I needed help. The health food stores had a couple of boxes of gluten-free baking mix, some rice and soy flours, and Hilda Cherry Hills's book *Good Food, Gluten Free*. Ms. Hills's book contained excellent advice on living, but frankly, the British recipes left me still searching for better taste.

I found an organization called the Gluten Intolerance Group (GIG), which met at our local university school of medicine. Besides providing medical and dietary information, members exchanged cooking hints and recounted horror stories about their own years BD (before diagnosis). I learned I was not alone. There are now estimated to be over a hundred thousand celiacs in the United States. This may be only the tip of the iceberg, for many doctors miss the diagnosis— a patient may not recount all his or her symptoms because they sound so diverse. Even more confusing for patient and doctor is the fact that celiac sprue symptoms can mimic many other disorders.

Finding how widespread the disease is gave me my start. Since then I have joined other celiac groups, become more informed from the increasing amount of literature and medical reports on celiac disease, and learned to cook with all the tasty flours available to us: both brown and white rice, sweet rice, potato and potato starch, soy, tapioca, cornstarch, corn flour, and cornmeal.

I've discovered it is possible to make good breads, cakes, cookies, and casseroles. I've even baked pizza and lasagne successfully. I stuff my turkey at Thanksgiving, eat plum pudding at Christmas and hot cross buns at Easter. I feed the family and any guests by my diet and they never suspect they are eating gluten-free foods. In fact, I am often asked for my recipes.

Today the newly diagnosed celiac is more fortunate than I was fifteen years ago. He or she can join national groups with a chapter nearby, has the choice of more cookbooks, and can find gluten-free bread in some health food stores or can order, by mail, diet breads, rolls, or cookies, and even a gluten-free pasta.

Scientists have made progress on the disease, but to date they have not come up with any way other than diet to stop the gliadin factor in gluten from damaging the small intestine. This damage can cause malabsorption of food and lead to possible anemia, malnutrition, calcium deficiency, or other problems for the celiac. A continued diet is still the only known way to regain health and stay in remission.

Now I am not even impatient for science to discover some miraculous cure for our disease. With my weight back to normal and my energy high, I eat well within the limitations of the gluten-free diet. I don't think of it as a diet for life, I consider it a prescription for living.

For more information about celiac disease or to find a group near you, contact one of these three national organizations:

Canadian Celiac Association, 6519-B Mississauga Road, Mississauga, Ontario L5T 1A6, Canada. Phone (416) 567-7195; FAX (416) 567-7191.

Celiac Sprue Association/United States of America (CSA/USA), P.O. Box 31700, Omaha, NE 68131-0700. Phone (402) 558-0600.

Gluten Intolerance Group of North America (GIG), P.O. Box 23053, Broadway Station, Seattle, WA 98102-0353. Phone (206) 325-6980.

REFERENCES

Hamilton, Helen Klusek, ed. director. *Professional Guide to Diseases.* Springhouse, PA: Springhouse Corporation, 1987.

Katz, S. "Dermatitis Herpetiformis, The Skin and the Gut." In *Annals of Internal Medicine* 93, no. 6 (December 1980): 857–74.

Schuffler, Michael. *Medical Facts About Celiac Sprue—New Research*. Address to the Gluten Intolerance Group, March 1981.

Seely, Stephen; Freed, David L. J.; Silverstone, Gerald A.; and Rippere, Vicky. *Diet-Related Diseases; the Modern Epidemic*. London, and Westport, CT: Croom Helm, AVI, 1985.

Winkelman, Eugene I. *The Many Faces of Sprue*. Address at CSA/USA national convention, October 1988.

THE HIDDEN GLUTENS

Once diagnosed, the patient suffering celiac disease naively assumes he will be able to recognize and eliminate wheat, oats, barley, and rye from his diet. He knows he will have to avoid breads and pastas and thinks he can simply read the label on everything else. What he doesn't realize is that some of the glutens hide under different names and labels, while some are not labeled at all.

Prescriptions

We expect medicines ordered by a doctor to heal us, but some use gluten as the filler for tablets or capsules. The doctor may be unaware of this or forget to mention it. It would be wise for the celiac to check all prescriptions (and even over-the-counter drugs) through his pharmacist. Many times a substitute brand will be gluten free; sometimes a different medication will have to be prescribed.

A larger number of prescriptions may use a lactose base and, since many celiacs suffer from lactose intolerance, these, too, can cause bloating, diarrhea, gas, or other distress.

Modified Food Starch

This ingredient listed on many foods labels could be corn, tapioca, or potato starch, which would be safe, but it could also be *wheat* starch. It is wise not to take chances. In the United States, if the label reads "starch," this signifies cornstarch and is thus safe.

Hydrolyzed Vegetable Protein (HVP)

The label does not tell which vegetable this protein is made from. It can be soy, corn, rice, peanuts, or casein from milk or *wheat*. If you wish to use a specific product you will have to check with the manufacturer to find the source of the HVP.

Distilled Vinegar

Products so labeled contain vinegar distilled from either wood or grain. Thus it is wise to avoid the product until you find out for sure whether the vinegar contains traces of gluten from the grain. (Wine vinegar, cider vinegar, and rice vinegar are all safe.) If you prefer a certain brand of mustard, mayonnaise, chili sauce, catsup, or the like, you might wish to write to the company to find out from which product their vinegar is distilled.

Flavorings and Extracts

Most of these on the grocery shelf are made with grain alcohol from a forbidden grain. You may wish to substitute ethel vanillin or dried orange or lemon peel for these flavors. Or find a line of gluten-free flavorings such as those produced by Bickford Flavors. These are available in health food stores or by mail order. (See page 221.)

Caramel Color

Caramel color can be made from dextrose (corn), invert sugar, lactose, molasses, sucrose (beet or cane). These are safely gluten free. But it may be made from gluten-containing malt syrup or starch hydrolysates, which can include wheat. If in doubt, write to the company.

Dextrin

Can be made from corn, potato, tapioca, rice, or *wheat*. It is wise to avoid dextrin unless it is labeled as corn dextrin, tapioca dextrin, and so on. To confuse one even more, malto-dextrin is made from cornstarch.

Triticale

This cereal grain found in some cereals and some flour mixtures is a cross of *wheat* and *rye* and contains gluten.

Rice Syrup

This flavoring can contain barley malt and might cause trouble for a celiac. If in doubt about the source of the rice syrup, write to the company for exact information.

Sirimi

This imitation seafood is created with a starch binder, in some cases cornstarch, in others *wheat* starch. Be sure to read the label before purchasing imitation crabmeat, shrimp, or scallops. Even more dangerous to those intolerant of wheat is the tendency in restaurants to mix imitation with real seafood in salads and other dishes. One should ask if there is sirimi in the seafood before ordering a crab, shrimp, or scallop dish in a restaurant or deli.

Candy

The ingredients in candy must be listed on the label, but currently the companies are not required to list any product that may dust the block the candy is rolled on for shaping. Some do use wheat flour. This was discovered when several celiacs in the Seattle Gluten Intolerance Group complained about symptoms of gluten poisoning after eating candy from a popular local company. The group adviser phoned the production manager of the company. She was told that the ingredients in the candy mixture were gluten free but, as the candy came down the conveyor belt, a dusting of wheat flour was added to make sure the candy would not stick. Thus, the puzzle of the illnesses was solved.

Instant or Powdered Coffee

There should be no gluten in powdered coffee, but some flavored coffees may contain the forbidden gluten. The author discovered that coffees made in England, especially, caused distress symptoms. Freeze-dried coffee seems less apt to cause problems.

Decaffeinated Coffee

Although the process of decaffeinating should not include the use of glutens, some celiac sufferers have felt distress on drinking decaffeinated coffee. The culprit could be the chemicals used in the process, rather than gluten. Water-processed decaffeinated coffee does not seem to provoke symptoms. The warning about flavored coffee should be observed here, too.

Tea

Tea is on the celiac's safe drink list, but some patients have complained that instant teas have induced discomfort. Again, it could be something else in the powdered product. Remember to read the labels on herb and flavored teas for additives that may contain gluten.

French Fries

French fried potatoes made at home or in a restaurant that cooks fresh-cut french fries in separate oil should be safe. But beware of any place that fries the potatoes in the same hot oil used for breaded products such as fish or chicken. Some of the gluten may transfer to the potatoes. Note also that some frozen potato products list wheat on the labels.

Hash Browns, Eggs, or Hamburger Patties

These are gluten free, but when ordering out in a restaurant, be sure they are cooked on a clean griddle, not on one that has been used for frying pancakes or browning hamburger buns. Again, the gluten can transfer to your food. Be sure your hamburger is pure meat and doesn't include any questionable additives.

Envelopes

Remember that some pastes and glues can contain wheat products. It will not take many licks on an envelope flap that contains a wheat paste before you start feeling distress. To be safe, buy a sponge-topped bottle made for sealing envelopes, fill it with water, and let it do the licking for you.

These are some of the more common hidden glutens. Once you become aware of them, you will find it far easier to avoid symptoms for which you previously could not pinpoint the cause.

REFERENCES

Bell, Louise; Hoffer, Miriam; and Hamilton, Richard. "Recommendation for Food of Questionable Acceptance for Patients with Celiac Disease." In *Journal of the Canadian Dietetic Association*, April 1981.

Hartsook, Elaine. Gluten Intolerance Group Newsletter, May 1988.

Liston, John. "From Seed to Shining Sea." Address on sirimi at Institute for Food Science, University of Washington, Seattle, November 1988.

Tyus, Frances J. "Additives . . . Knowing Can Make Your Diet More Flexible." Paper delivered at National CSA/USA convention, October 1988.

Winter, Ruth. *A Consumer's Dictionary of Food Additives*. Newly Revised Edition. New York: Crown Publishers, 1984.

COOKING WITH GLUTEN-FREE FLOURS

The first baking I tried with gluten-free flour produced a powdery, tasteless muffin that even my grandson rejected. I ate the thing because I was hungry for a bread substitute.

Since that first attempt, I have learned that although gluten-free flours do not act like wheat, baked products can turn out fine-textured, springy, and moist if one follows a few simple rules and understands the limitations of each flour.

Because the flours do not contain gluten, the "stretch" factor, baked products tend to be dry and crumbly unless some other stretch factor is added. This can be extra egg, cottage or ricotta cheese, extra leavening, and, in yeast breads, the addition of xanthan or guar gum.

Flours without gluten also seem to produce better products when used in combination. One can use white rice flour plus tapioca for a fine-textured cake; brown or white rice flour plus potato starch and tapioca in breads; rice flour plus soy in fruit-filled cakes or waffles; and potato starch flour plus cornstarch in pizza dough. This blending of flours is probably much like the various wheat flours blended by mills for different uses. But we must blend our own and experiment with ratios to achieve perfection in our baking.

For many of my recipes I keep on hand a combination of two parts rice flour (white), two-thirds part potato starch flour, and one-third part tapioca flour. I call this my GF (gluten-free) flour mixture and often use it as the flour when converting a wheat recipe to a gluten-free one. Then I add extra egg and leavening. Many times this is all that is needed for conversion. Other changes might be replacing oil with mayonnaise or butter with shortening.

If you haven't worked with these flours before, it's easiest to start with simple recipes to satisfy the longing for something besides rice crackers. But it won't be long before you can turn out baked products that nondieting friends will enjoy as well. For thickening agents in gravies, puddings, and so on, rice flour, potato starch, tapioca, and cornstarch all work well. I use rice flour in all my gravies, potato starch and sweet rice flour in cream sauces and soups, tapioca and cornstarch in pies and fruit dishes.

Because these do not exchange in equal quantity with wheat flour, it is best to understand what each flour is.

White Rice Flour

A standby for my cooking. A white flour milled from polished white rice, this has a bland flavor that does not distort the taste of the baked product. I often combine it with another gluten-free flour because baked items made with only rice flour tend to have a rather grainy texture. This keeps well so it can be bought in quantity. You can order it through suppliers listed on pages 221–222 or buy it in twenty-pound boxes from bakeries, which use it to dust baking pans. A call to a nearby bakery supply firm will let you know if any rice flour is available near you. To avoid contamination from gluten flours in the bakery, one should purchase only unopened boxes.

Brown Rice Flour

A flour milled from the unpolished rice, this is bran-flavored, and great for some breads, muffins, and cookies where the bran taste is desired. This flour is high in nutrient value but, because there are oils in the bran, it has a much shorter shelf life and tends to become stronger tasting as it ages. Purchase fresh flour and store it in the freezer for longer life.

Rice Bran

As the name implies, this is the bran flour obtained from polishing brown rice. It rates high in minerals, vitamin B, vitamin E, protein, and fiber. I often add it to cookies, muffins, and some breads. This, too, has a short shelf life because of the high amount of oils, so it is best to buy it as needed. Don't store it for long except in the freezer.

Sweet Rice Flour

This flour, made from a glutinous rice often called "sticky rice," is an excellent thickening agent. It is especially good for sauces that are to be refrigerated or frozen, as it inhibits separation of the liquids.

Rice Polish

This is a soft, fluffy, cream-colored flour made from the hulls of brown rice. Like rice bran, it has a high concentration of minerals and B vitamins. And like rice bran, it has a short shelf life.

Potato Starch Flour

A very fine white flour with a bland taste, excellent for baking when combined with other flours. This is also a good thickening agent for cream soups but it must be mixed with water first, and you should use about half the amount you would need of a wheat flour. This keeps well and can be bought in quantity.

Potato Flour

Do not confuse this with potato starch. This is a heavy flour with a definite potato taste. I use very little of it. When it is called for in a recipe, it can often be replaced with Potato Buds or mashed potatoes.

Tapioca Flour

A very light, white, velvety flour obtained from the cassava root, this imparts a bit of "chew" to baked goods and is excellent used in small quantities with other flours for most baking. I have also used it in almost equal parts in recipes where "chew" is desirable, such as English muffins, French bread, and pizza crusts. This keeps well, so it can be bought in quantity.

Soy Flour

A yellow flour having high protein and fat content, this has a nutty flavor and is most successful when used in combination with other flours in baked products that contain fruit, nuts, or chocolate. It also is excellent in waffles for its distinctive taste. Purchase this in small quantities, as it, too, has a shorter shelf life than white rice flour and potato starch.

Cornstarch

A refined starch obtained from corn. It makes a clear thickening for puddings and fruit sauces. It is also used in combination with other flours in baking.

Corn Flour

A flour milled from corn, this can be blended with cornmeal when making cornbreads and corn muffins.

Xanthan Gum

A powder milled from the dried cell coat of a microorganism called *Xanthomonas campestris* grown under laboratory conditions. It works as an excellent substitute for the gluten in yeast breads made from flours other than wheat. The only drawback about using xanthan gum is that it is difficult to find. It can be ordered by mail (see page 222 for the company that sells it), and some celiac groups have banded together to purchase it in quantity to divide among their members and to provide at cost to others. To make excellent gluten-free baked breads and pastas it is well worth the trouble to secure.

Guar Gum

A powder derived from the seed of the plant *Cyamopsis tetragono-lobus*. This can often be purchased in health food stores, but, since it has a high fiber content and is sometimes used as a laxative, one should be aware that when used in baking it can cause distress to some people whose digestive systems are sensitive.

Principles of Substitution

As a general rule, you can use the following formula. For each cup of wheat flour called for in a recipe substitute one of the following:

> 7/8 cup rice flour
> 5/8 cup potato starch flour
> 1 cup soy flour plus 1/4 cup potato starch flour
> 1/2 cup soy flour plus 1/2 cup potato starch flour
> 1 cup corn flour
> 1 scant cup fine cornmeal
> 1 cup of the GF flour mixture I suggest on page 10

These different flours can be purchased in health food stores, in some supermarkets, and by mail order (see pages 221–222).

White rice flour and brown rice flour are interchangeable except in some recipes where the white color is important. I have specified one or the other in a few recipes.

TIME-SAVING TIPS
FOR THE COOK

Cooking from scratch, as most gluten-free recipes require, takes extra time for the cook, but there are shortcuts to make it easier.

Mix flour combinations ahead of time and store in canisters or coffee cans. I have given on page 10 a 3-part flour mix I use in many of my baking recipes. I always keep this on hand. I also double the amount of dry mixture for the True Yeast Bread and keep that stored (tightly sealed) for the next baking, thus saving time and mess on a future baking day. Pancake and muffin mix flours, sugar, and leavening can be mixed ahead of time and stored, needing only the addition of eggs, liquid, and oil at the last minute.

Crush gluten-free cereals in a plastic bag. This saves a mess in the kitchen. Roll with a rolling pin and then, if you are using the cereal as a pie crust, add the melted margarine or butter and sugar to the cereal in the bag and blend by shaking. Dump into pie tin and pat out. No bowl to clean.

Save all stale GF bread or baking mistakes. Use them for stuffing, casseroles, or dry them in the oven and turn into crumbs with a food processor or blender. Freeze these to pull out later to use in crumb crusts or cookie recipes that call for crumbs. If you want them to taste like graham cracker crumbs, add a bit of cinnamon and sugar.

When making gravy, double the amount and save the extra to freeze and use in casseroles. Make gravy using white rice flour browned in the drippings just as you would any wheat flour. Add water to achieve a thick gravy and thin with milk or nondairy liquid to the desired consistency.

Freeze single portions of GF leftovers on small microwave frozen food trays. Pull these out for the gluten-intolerant diner when a dish containing gluten is served to the rest of the family.

Make ahead and freeze GF cream soups and sauces in 1-cup portions. Use these handy premeasured portions in recipes that call for cream soups and sauces. Recipes for these will be found on pages 142–144 and 185–187.

Use as many prepared foods as possible. Many frostings, sauces, and seasoning mixes are safely gluten free. There are rice and corn pastas available on the grocery shelves, or order pastas by mail from suppliers. (See list on pages 221–222.)

Buttermilk for baking—and many GF recipes call for this—can be kept on hand by storing a can or box of powdered buttermilk on the kitchen shelf. Or substitute the equivalent amount of liquid by adding 1 tablespoon of lemon juice to each cup of milk and let stand 5 minutes.

Keep on hand a good supply of rice crackers that are now being sold in many supermarkets. The small, round oriental cracker is great for hors d'oeuvres or snacking. The thin cracker put out by Hol•Grain makes a thin sandwich using cheese, ham, or a mixed spread. Crispy Cakes, about the size and shape of a graham cracker, made by Pacific Rice Products, have several GF flavors and are thick enough to make a tasty open-faced sandwich. They can also be crushed and used as crumbs for baking. The new Minicrispys, also by Pacific Rice, have flavors that taste like cookies. Weight Watchers Crispbread in harvest rice flavor is also gluten free. This is a rice and soy flour cracker with an excellent flavor.

The microwave, freezer, food processor, and heavy-duty mixer save work and time and so are well worth the investment. Several celiacs have written that they also own a flour mill for grinding their own flours from the whole grain. This could save money, time waiting for orders to arrive, and the possibility of contamination at a mill that also grinds wheat flours.

TRAVELING AND
DINING OUT

Eating out on our diet may seem, at first, an exercise in frustration, with all those delectable dishes on the menu that we can't eat. But, just as the diabetic learns to avoid sugar and the overweight shun the high-calorie dishes, the celiac learns to recognize gluten and avoid it.

It's easy to wave away the bread and to refrain from ordering pasta, stuffed meats, or casserole dishes. But, from there on, the menu should be discussed with the serving person or chef. Is the steak marinated in a sauce that could contain gluten before being broiled? Is the liver or other meat floured before grilling? Does the salad contain croutons, and the salad dressing wheat or distilled vinegar? Was the turkey stuffed before roasting, or was the stuffing baked separately? Is there wheat in the soy sauce in that Chinese dish?

Fifteen years ago, as a newly diagnosed celiac, I was embarrassed to ask questions that might send my waitress or waiter back to the kitchen several times, and as a result I often received food that I had to leave untouched. Now I ask. I explain the reason for the questions, and most serving people have been obliging, sometimes bringing the cook to the table or taking me to the cook. I give the restaurant four stars in my book when the cook understands and makes me a plate that looks great, tastes great, and is completely gluten free. And the cook gets five stars when others in the restaurant look at my plate and wonder where I found *that* on the menu.

It's easy for the cook to prepare you a good meal if you ask for grilled or plain roasted (no "aux juice" or bouillon-basted) meat, or grilled or poached fish, with potatoes (parsley-buttered or baked), with some vegetable or fruit.

Another trick is to look at the appetizer list. What's wrong with stuffed potatoes, or a kettle of clams in their own broth; avocado stuffed with seafood (as long as there's no sirimi in it), or a serving of potato skins with cheese and bacon bits as a main course? If you have taken along your rice crackers or, better yet, some of the bread sticks you'll find on page 31, you won't envy your dinner companion that chicken fried steak, stuffed pork chop, or even scalloped oysters.

This is simple for you if the restaurant has a full menu, but even fast-food places can provide a good meal. I've ordered a "sandwich" without the bread and had a full serving of ham or turkey with lettuce and tomato or cheese. When ordering soup to go with it, I make sure it doesn't contain barley or pasta or have a wheat thickener or, horrors, come from a can. Try hamburgers without the bun, french fries and salads at McDonald's, or head for the salad bar at the nearest pizza parlor.

If all else fails, turn to the breakfast menu. An omelet tastes good any time and one stuffed with meat and vegetables can be a full meal.

These are only a few suggestions to get you over those first visits to a restaurant. You'll probably find, after a short time, that any eating establishment can provide a good gluten-free meal with a few suggestions from you and an obliging cook.

The rules above can be followed for any eating out, whether for a single meal or while traveling. But for anything longer than a day trip you might want to pack a "survival kit." For me this is a supply of rice crackers, cheese (single slices wrapped separately), dried or fresh fruit, cookies (the Peanut Butter Drops on page 51 are great!), and some candy. I have carried this kit on a train through China and it's helped me survive long plane trips, bus excursions, and even a breakdown in the British Midlands.

By far the best way for the celiac to vacation is camping, where you carry and cook your own food, whether you rough it in a tent or travel by trailer or motor home. When you go to a resort, rent a condo rather than a hotel room and eat some meals in.

For more extensive traveling, the cruise ship is the easiest on our diet. Take along a few of your breads and cookies and talk over your diet with the maître d' as soon as you go aboard. If there is no refrigerator in your stateroom, he will put your food in one of the kitchen refrigerators and your waiter will bring items out as needed.

I always keep a supply of rice crackers in my stateroom either for snacks or for taking with me when we leave the ship for a day's shore excursion.

Eating on planes can be a bit more tricky. Although some airlines do claim to provide gluten-free meals, I have discovered that it isn't always wise to trust the travel agent. On a long trip to England I ordered gluten-free meals and, to my astonishment, found that I was expected to eat green salads for breakfast, lunch, and dinner! Well, it *was* gluten free; but I was hungry when we arrived at Heathrow. After that, I started carrying the survival packet with me. Many airline meals have a gluten-free main dish, salad, and a fruit, and you can supplement the meal with your survival extras.

For foreign travel, your packet of extras could include dried soups, canned tuna and chicken, a small jar of peanut butter, and some of the freeze-dried foods provided for backpackers and campers. Most foreign hotel rooms provide a hot kettle or hot water so you can easily make up a cup of soup and have a rice cracker sandwich to go with it. Add a sweet and you're ready to go exploring. You won't be the only one doing this. Many experienced travelers have learned these tricks to save time, money, and disappointment when they discover they've reached a hotel ten minutes after the dining room closed.

As for that continental breakfast, let someone else eat your croissant and pile your rice cracker with the butter and jam provided. At the beginning of the trip, you might want to enjoy a few English Muffins, page 104. They are great travelers.

If you follow these few suggestions, eating out while traveling can be easy. And, as a bonus, when the food is gone, there will be extra space in your luggage for those souvenirs.

BREADS

YEAST BREADS

True Yeast Bread 25
Hamburger Buns 26
Sticky Pecan Rolls 27
Celiac Sourdough
    Bread 27
Tapioca Bread 29
Donna Jo's French Bread
    (an almost sugar-free,
    single-rising bread) 30
Bread Sticks 31
Egg Sesame Bread (a lactose-
    free, soy-free bread) 31
Single-Rising Coffee
    Bread 32
    Julekaka 33
    Cinnamon-Nut
    Bread 33
Dilly Casserole Bread 33

QUICK-RISING BREADS

Potato-Rice Sponge
    Bread 34
Potato Quick Bread 35
Best Banana Bread 35
Hawaiian Tea Bread 36
Apricot Bread 37
Pumpkin Bread 38
Lentil Sesame Bread 38

SMALL BREADS

Quick and Easy
    Muffins 40
Blueberry or Cranberry
    Muffins 40
Rice Bran Muffins 40
Kasha (Buckwheat)
    Muffins 41

YEAST BREADS

There is no quick trip to the bakery or the baked goods section of the local grocery store for the gluten intolerant when he craves bread. For him, eating those loaves made with wheat, oats, or rye would be like taking a daily dose of poison.

There are a few bakeries that specialize in gluten-free breads. Some that sell bread by mail order are listed at the back of this book. Because they usually delete sugar, eggs, and milk to make the breads suitable for those intolerances also, these breads leave a lot to be desired in the taste department. I use them mostly for casseroles or as toast, since they are better heated and slathered with jam or marmalade.

You can settle for the egg-leavened loaf breads, the nut or fruit breads, or the muffins included in this chapter, all of which are quick to fix. But if your mouth still waters for the remembered flavor of yeasty-tasting, chewy breads, you may still enjoy them if you are willing to take the time and trouble to bake your own.

In the following pages you will find the yeast bread recipes that proved most successful in my own kitchen. And, believe me, I had plenty of failures before I came up with these. The pile of bread crumbs I pulverized in my blender and used later in other dishes would have kept an army of mice happy for years. I had never attempted bread before I was diagnosed, so at first I placed all blame for failure on my ignorance. I now realize that only a few recipes are successful using gluten-free flours.

Some of the secrets of making successful gluten-free yeast breads are:

Follow the mixing directions carefully.

Use fresh yeast, not quick rising. I prefer fresh yeast cakes for their flavor and easy digestibility, but since they are often hard to find, you may substitute 1 tablespoon dry yeast granules for each yeast cake in the recipe.

Let bread rise in warm place. Putting the pan in an oven that has been turned to 200° for a few minutes and then turned off before you put in the dough works well. Another trick is to set the mixing bowl in a pan of warm water.

The water for softening the yeast must be lukewarm only. Too hot will kill the yeast; too cold, the yeast will not work. Test with a thermometer (105°–115°) or put a drop on the inside of your wrist, as one tests milk for a baby's bottle. The water should contain some sugar.

A heavy-duty mixer (such as KitchenAid) helps mix our bread. The dough is softer and stickier than gluten bread dough and cannot be kneaded by hand.

Xanthan gum is necessary for all the yeast recipes to help make the breads springy and chewy. It replaces, in part, the gluten that rice and potato flours lack. See the back of the book for the name of a supplier from whom this may be ordered. Guar gum may be substituted for the xanthan gum in equal amounts, but guar gum, often sold as a laxative, may cause distress to some who eat the bread.

Adding extra protein in the form of eggs, dry milk solids, or *cottage cheese helps the yeast work.*

1 teaspoon of vinegar added to any yeast bread recipe helps the yeast work and develops flavor.

Baking the bread in small pans (2¹/₂" × 5") or muffin tins will often turn out a product with better texture.

Some recipes in this section call for a mixture of gluten-free flours I keep on hand. The formula for that GF flour mix is:

2 parts white rice flour
²/₃ part potato starch flour
¹/₃ part tapioca flour

TRUE YEAST BREAD

When gluten intolerance was first recognized, there were no recipes for a yeast bread without wheat. There still are very few that turn out a product that smells, slices, and tastes like leavened wheat bread. This recipe, adapted from one created in the nutrition department of the University of Washington School of Medicine, makes an excellent bread.

3 cups GF flour mix	1/2 cup lukewarm water
1/4 cup sugar	1 1/2 yeast cakes, or
3 1/2 teaspoons xanthan gum	1 1/2 tablespoons yeast granules
2/3 cup dry milk powder*	1/4 cup shortening
1 1/2 teaspoons salt	1 1/4 cups water
2 teaspoons sugar	1 teaspoon vinegar
	3 eggs

Combine flour, sugar, xanthan gum, milk powder, and salt in bowl of heavy-duty mixer. Use your strongest beaters.

Dissolve the 2 teaspoons of sugar in the 1/2 cup of lukewarm water and mix in the yeast. Set aside while you combine the shortening and 1 1/4 cups water in saucepan and heat until shortening melts.

Turn mixer on low. Blend dry ingredients and slowly add shortening and water mixture and the vinegar. Blend, then add eggs. This mixture should feel slightly warm.

Pour the yeast mixture into the ingredients in the bowl and beat at highest speed for 2 minutes.

Place mixing bowl in a warm place, cover with plastic wrap and a towel, and let the dough rise approximately 1 to 1 1/2 hours or until doubled.

Return to the mixer and beat on high for 3 minutes.

Spoon the dough into 3 small (2 1/2" × 5") greased loaf pans or 1 large one. Use muffin tins and bake any remainder as small rolls. Or make all rolls (approximately 18).

*For the lactose intolerant, see page x for powdered baby formula substitutions. Use equal amounts.

Let rise until the dough is slightly above top of pan. Bake in pre-heated 400° oven for 10 minutes. Place foil over bread and bake large loaves 50 minutes longer, small loaves slightly less time, and rolls about 25 minutes.

NOTES: The dough texture will seem more like cookie dough than bread dough, so don't be alarmed. Bread is better when baked in small loaf pans and delicious in rolls.

I have successfully doubled the recipe to turn out 2 large loaves plus 18 rolls in the muffin tins or 3 small $2^{1}/_{2}$" × 5" loaves plus 24 rolls. The bread freezes well. For convenience, slice before freezing.

This bread may be made with either brown or white rice flour in the GF flour mix.

HAMBURGER BUNS

Follow the recipe above for True Yeast Bread but after the first rising, shape some or all as follows:

Use 4" English muffin rings as forms. Grease them inside and place on well-greased cookie sheet. Or make your own forms for containing the dough by taking a sheet of foil (about 10 inches torn from roll), folding it in half, then half again and again until you get a strong strip slightly over 1 inch wide. Tape the ends together with masking tape to form a circle. Make as many as you desire, grease the inside, and place on greased cookie sheets. Pour your bread dough into these forms after the second beating, filling the forms only half full.

Let rise to double in height and bake in preheated 375° oven for 20 to 25 minutes.

STICKY PECAN ROLLS

Follow the recipe for True Yeast Bread but after the first rising, instead of putting in pans, place about 2 cups of dough on buttered wax paper. With well-greased hands pat it out to about 1/3 inch thick in a rectangular shape. Then:

Spread with a mixture of 1/4 cup (1/2 stick) softened butter and 1/4 cup brown sugar.
Sprinkle on 1/2 cup chopped pecans.

Form a roll, carefully working the sticky dough from the waxed paper. Don't worry if it doesn't become smooth or look perfect.

Seal the roll and then slice in about 1 1/4-inch pieces. Put pieces in muffin tins greased with an extra dab of butter on the bottom and let rise.

Bake in preheated 375° oven for 20 minutes.

CELIAC SOURDOUGH BREAD

A bread that is springy, chewy, tasty, crusty, and good both hot and cold. This recipe is a variation of one Margaret Powers offers in her excellent book Gluten Free and Good!

The bread begins with a sourdough starter.

STARTER

1 cake fresh yeast
1 cup lukewarm water
1 1/2 cups rice flour

Dissolve the yeast in the warm water and let sit 10 to 15 minutes. Slowly add the flour and mix well with a wooden spoon.

Place in a clean jar or crock (never in metal) and allow to sit at room temperature until fermented and bubbly. If in a warm room, this may require only 15 minutes.

When bubbly and risen a little, cover and refrigerate. Starter is now ready for use. It should be the consistency of thick pancake batter when ready to use. It is best used within several weeks.

BREAD

Use nonmetal pans and utensils as much as possible when mixing this bread. Since this is a stiff dough, you will need a heavy-duty mixer and a bread hook.

3 cups GF flour mix	2 teaspoons xanthan
1/2 cup sugar	gum
3/4 teaspoon salt	3/4 cup sourdough starter
1 cup powdered dry milk,	1 cup quite warm water
or powdered baby	3 eggs
formula, page x	1 1/2 cups cottage cheese

Place flour mix, sugar, salt, powdered milk, and xanthan gum in mixing bowl and blend together on very low speed.

In another bowl, beat together the sourdough starter, water, eggs, and cottage cheese. Mix them slowly into the flour with bread hook of mixer. Beat for about 4 minutes.

Cover and let rise until double in bulk. Don't hurry. This may take up to 1 1/2 hours.

Beat again for 5 minutes. Fill greased bread or muffin pans three-quarters full. Let rise until dough is almost to top of pans, about 40 minutes.

Place in preheated 350° oven and watch to see when dough rises to top of pans and rounds on top (about 10 minutes), then increase heat to 400° to finish baking.

FEEDING STARTER

After each use, the remaining starter must be fed to provide enough quantity for the next use and to reactivate it.

1 cup starter
1 cup warm water
1 1/2 cups rice flour

Mix together in glass jar or crock. Let stand until doubled in bulk. Starter is ready when it has bubbled and mounded up. Refrigerate until next use.

TAPIOCA BREAD

For a fine, white, springy-textured bread try this rice and tapioca flour mixture. You will find it tastes like wheat flour breads.

2 cups rice flour	1 1/2 yeast cakes, or 1 1/2
1 1/2 cups tapioca	tablespoons dry yeast
flour	granules
1/4 cup sugar	1/2 cup lukewarm water
3 1/2 teaspoons xanthan	2 teaspoons sugar
gum	1/4 cup shortening
2/3 cup dry milk	1 1/4 cups water
powder	1 teaspoon vinegar
1 1/2 teaspoons salt	3 large eggs

Combine flours, sugar, xanthan gum, milk powder, and salt in the large bowl of a heavy-duty mixer. In a separate bowl, break yeast into the lukewarm water with the 2 teaspoons of sugar added, and let dissolve. Melt shortening in 1 1/4 cups of water in saucepan.

Pour shortening mixture and vinegar into dry ingredients and blend on low. Add eggs and beat a few seconds. Add the dissolved yeast. Beat at highest speed for 2 minutes.

Place the mixing bowl, tightly covered with plastic wrap, in a warm place and let rise until dough has doubled, approximately 1 to 1 1/2 hours.

Return dough to mixer and beat 3 minutes. Spoon dough into 2 small greased loaf pans or 1 large one, plus a few spoonfuls in greased muffin tins to bake as rolls. Let dough rise again for approximately

1 hour. Bake in preheated 400° oven for 10 minutes. Place foil over the bread to keep it from turning too dark and bake 50 minutes more for the large loaf, about 15 minutes less for the small loaves, and about 25 minutes for the rolls.

DONNA JO'S FRENCH BREAD

(an almost sugar-free, single-rising bread)

This recipe was developed by one of my testers who, upon tasting Tapioca Bread, wondered if she couldn't create a French bread texture by increasing the egg whites and cutting the sugar. A real success. This is so good your friends won't believe it is gluten free. But this mix, with very little sugar to keep the yeast working, needs to be kept extra warm.

This bread is best baked at a time of low humidity. Damp weather seems to make the bread soggy.

2 cups white rice flour
1 1/4 cups tapioca flour
1 1/2 teaspoons salt
2/3 cup dry powdered milk
3 1/2 teaspoons xanthan gum
1 1/2 teaspoons sugar
1 3/4 cups warm water

2 yeast cakes, or 2 tablespoons dry yeast granules
1 teaspoon vinegar
4 egg whites at room temperature
Optional: 1 egg white, beaten

Into bowl of mixer place flours, salt, milk powder, and xanthan gum. Add the sugar to the warm water and crumble in the yeast. This will not foam up, since there is very little sugar to make it work. Add the yeast to the dry ingredients and blend with mixer. Add the vinegar and mix. Add the egg whites. Beat 2 or 3 minutes.

To form loaves, spoon dough onto greased cookie sheets in 2 long French loaf shapes or spoon into greased French bread pans. Slash diagonally every few inches. Brush with beaten egg white if desired. Cover the loaves and let rise in a warm place until doubled (up to 1 hour). Bake 30 minutes in preheated oven at 400°. *Makes 2 loaves.*

BREAD STICKS

Instead of forming loaves, use the French Bread recipe above and spoon the dough into a plastic freezer bag with 1/2 inch of one corner cut off. Squeeze the dough in strips onto 2 greased cookie sheets. The recipe will make about a dozen 12-inch sticks or two dozen 6-inch sticks.

Let rise until doubled (up to 1 hour), and bake about 20 to 25 minutes in preheated 400° oven.

EGG SESAME BREAD
(a lactose-free, soy-free bread)

A boon for those who are both lactose- and soy-intolerant so cannot substitute the soy-based powdered baby formula for the dry powdered milk in the other bread recipes. This is an excellent-tasting bread with a rich flavor, so it can be eaten with just butter or in any kind of sandwich.

1 1/2 tablespoons sesame seeds
2 cups rice flour
1 3/4 cups tapioca flour
1/4 cup sugar
3 1/2 teaspoons xanthan gum
1 1/2 teaspoons salt
1 1/2 yeast cakes, or 1 1/2 tablespoons of dry yeast granules

1/2 cup lukewarm water
2 teaspoons sugar
1/4 cup shortening
1 1/4 cups water
1 teaspoon vinegar
3 eggs, at room temperature
2 egg yolks

Brown sesame seeds in heavy skillet on medium heat. Set aside. Combine flours, 1/4 cup sugar, xanthan gum, and salt in bowl of mixer. Blend. In a separate bowl, dissolve yeast in warm water to which the 2 teaspoons of sugar have been added. In saucepan, melt shortening in the 1 1/4 cups water.

Pour shortening mixture into dry ingredients, add vinegar, and blend on low. Add eggs and egg yolks, beating slightly. The mixture should be slightly warm. Add yeast water and beat 2 minutes on high. Stir in most of the toasted sesame seeds, reserving a pinch or two for the top.

Place the mixing bowl, tightly covered with plastic wrap, in a warm place and let dough rise until doubled, about 1 to 1 1/2 hours.

Return dough to mixer and beat for 3 minutes. Spoon dough into three 2 1/2" × 5" greased loaf pans or 1 large one plus a few spoonfuls in greased muffin tins to bake as rolls. Sprinkle with the remaining sesame seeds. Let dough rise again in a warm place until doubled, approximately 1 hour.

Bake in preheated 400° oven for 10 minutes. Place foil over the bread to keep it from turning too dark and bake 50 minutes more for the large loaf, about 15 minutes less for the small loaves, and about 25 minutes if you have made rolls.

This bread freezes well. Cool and slice before freezing.

SINGLE-RISING COFFEE BREAD

An easy-to-make, fine-grained sweet yeast bread that is good with just butter or with jam. This bread will take the addition of raisins, spices, or nuts for an entirely different taste. The use of both baking powder and yeast as leavening agents gives it an unusual flavor.

2 cups GF flour mix	1/2 cup shortening
4 teaspoons baking powder	1 yeast cake, or 1
1/4 cup sugar	tablespoon dry yeast
1/4 cup powdered milk, or	granules
powdered baby formula,	3/4 cup warm water
page x	1 tablespoon sugar
3/4 teaspoon salt	2 eggs at room
2 teaspoons xanthan gum	temperature

Place flour, baking powder, sugar, dry milk, salt, and xanthan gum in large bowl of mixer. Cut in the shortening. In a separate bowl, dissolve yeast in warm water with 1 tablespoon of sugar. Add with the eggs to the flour mixture. Beat 5 minutes with bread hook. The dough will be very thick.

Grease hands and knead dough using a rice-floured board. Pat into round shape about 8 inches in diameter and approximately 2 inches thick at center.

Let stand 40 minutes or more until doubled in size.

Bake on a greased cookie sheet in preheated 375° oven for 40 minutes covered with aluminum foil to prevent dark crust.

NOTE: Those who are both lactose and soy intolerant can eliminate the powdered milk and replace the water and powdered milk with 3/4 cup fruit juice (orange, pear, or other). Add 2 extra egg yolks for protein. Remember to add the extra tablespoon of sugar to the juice to help the yeast work.

JULEKAKA: Turn the above bread into a Christmas loaf by adding 1 teaspoon dried orange rind and 1 cup chopped candied fruit.

CINNAMON-NUT BREAD: Another variation can be made by adding 1 teaspoon cinnamon to the flours and stirring in 1/2 to 1 cup chopped nuts at the end of the beating.

DILLY CASSEROLE BREAD

This is an unusual and excitingly flavored bread made in a round shape and baked in a casserole. It is wonderful with just butter and makes a fine accompaniment to soups. It also makes a hearty sandwich with strong-tasting fillings like ham, cheese, or corned beef.

1 yeast cake, or 1 packet dry yeast granules
1/4 cup warm water
2 tablespoons sugar
1 cup creamed cottage cheese
2 eggs, at room temperature
2 teaspoons dill seed

1/2 teaspoon salt
1/4 teaspoon baking soda
1 tablespoon butter or margarine
1 tablespoon instant minced onion
2 cups GF flour mix
2 teaspoons xanthan gum

Soften yeast in the warm water to which the sugar has been added. Warm cottage cheese to lukewarm.

Combine in bowl of mixer all the ingredients except the flours and xanthan gum. Add the flours and xanthan gum slowly, beating after each addition until you have a stiff dough. Leave in bowl and let rise in warm place (85° to 90°) until doubled, 50 to 60 minutes.

Stir the dough down and turn it into greased 8″ round casserole. Let rise again until light, 30 to 40 minutes. Then bake in oven pre-heated to 350° for 40 to 50 minutes, until golden. Brush with soft butter.

QUICK-RISING BREADS

POTATO-RICE SPONGE BREAD

This is a fine eating bread with jam or spreads. It is good toasted or used for french toast. Since it contains no yeast, it is a good substitute if you cannot tolerate yeast products.

6 eggs, at room temperature	1/2 cup rice flour
2 1/2 tablespoons sugar	1 teaspoon salt
3/4 cup potato starch flour	2 teaspoons baking powder

Separate eggs. In large bowl, beat egg whites until mounds form. Then beat in the sugar a tablespoon at a time. In another bowl, beat egg yolks until light, creamy, and fluffy, approximately 5 minutes at high speed.

Sift together the flours, salt, and baking powder. Sprinkle about one-third of the flour mixture over the whites; fold together gently until well mixed; repeat two times. Carefully fold beaten egg yolks into flour mixture until well blended.

Pour batter into coated nonstick 8″ × 4″ × 3″ loaf pan. Bake in preheated 350° oven for 45 to 50 minutes. Cool 1 hour before removing from pan. Allow to cool 3 hours before slicing.

POTATO QUICK BREAD

This nonyeast bread is heavier than the preceding one but excellent for toast and open-faced sandwiches, especially if they are to be microwaved or heated under the broiler. Use toppings like cheese, tuna and mayonnaise, or others with moistness and strong flavor.

1 cup milk or buttermilk	2 cups potato starch flour
2 eggs	2 teaspoons baking powder
2 tablespoons sugar	1 teaspoon salt
2 tablespoons vegetable oil	Optional: 1 teaspoon xanthan gum

Scald sweet milk (if used), and set aside to cool. Buttermilk does not need to be scalded.

Separate eggs. Beat whites until stiff. In a separate bowl, beat yolks. Add cooled milk, sugar, and oil to beaten yolks.

Sift together flour, baking powder, salt, and xanthan gum and add to the yolk mixture. Mix well. Then gently fold in egg whites.

Pour batter into 2 greased 8″ × 4″ bread pans. Bake in preheated 350° oven for 40 minutes.

BEST BANANA BREAD

After trying many banana breads that crumbled on cutting, I discovered a combination of flours, including soy, that turns out a firm loaf. The texture is fine and the flavor is nutty banana without being too sweet.

1 cup soy flour	1/3 cup shortening
1/2 cup potato starch flour	2/3 cup sugar
1/4 cup rice flour	2 eggs, well beaten
3/4 teaspoon baking soda	1/2 cup mashed banana
1 1/4 teaspoons cream of tartar	Optional: 1/2 cup chopped nuts
1/2 teaspoon salt	

Sift the flours, baking soda, cream of tartar, and salt together. Set aside.

In a mixing bowl, cream shortening. Gradually add the sugar, beating until light and fluffy. Add the well-beaten eggs. Beat well. Add the dry ingredients alternately with the mashed banana, a small amount at a time, beating after each addition until smooth.

Stir in the chopped nuts if desired. Pour into well-greased 8″ × 4″ loaf pan and bake for 1 hour in oven preheated to 350°.

HAWAIIAN TEA BREAD

This "party" bread with a hint of sunny tropical isles can be served in place of cake. And it can be served to those with not only gluten and lactose intolerance but, with a slight change in recipe, to those who can't have eggs. But hide some to save for yourself.

1/3 cup (2/3 stick) margarine, softened	1 teaspoon baking powder
2/3 cup honey	1/2 teaspoon baking soda
2 eggs, beaten, or 1/4 cup vegetable oil	1 cup grated coconut, sweetened or unsweetened
2 tablespoons water	Optional: 1 cup chopped walnuts
1/2 teaspoon vanilla	4 ripe bananas, sliced thin
1 cup rice flour	
1/2 cup rice polish	

In a large bowl, cream margarine. Beat while adding honey in fine stream. Beat in eggs, or oil if you are allergic to eggs. Stir in water and vanilla. In a separate bowl, sift together rice flour, rice polish, baking powder, and baking soda. Add coconut and walnuts (if used).

Add dry ingredients alternately with bananas to the creamed mixture, folding only until everything is moistened. Spoon into greased 9″ × 5″ loaf pan. Bake for 55 minutes in preheated 350° oven. Allow to cool in pan for 5 minutes before removing.

APRICOT BREAD

A different fruit-flavored bread for those who are tired of banana. The texture of this is slightly grainier than that of the banana bread, but the flavor more than compensates. It is good plain as a coffee cake, with just butter, or, for a lunch box treat, serve with cream cheese or other mild-tasting cheese.

If you prefer, you may eliminate the soy flour and use 2 cups of rice flour. I like the taste with the soy added, but the recipe will turn out well either way.

1 cup apricot purée	1/2 teaspoon baking soda
1/2 cup sugar	1 teaspoon salt
2 tablespoons shortening	1 tablespoon grated orange
2 eggs	peel
1 1/2 cups rice flour	1/2 cup orange juice
1/2 cup soy flour	1 cup chopped nuts
1 tablespoon baking powder	

Purée apricots in blender. Set aside. (I use canned apricots, drained, or use dried apricots that you have cooked and drained.)

Cream sugar and shortening. Add eggs and puréed apricots. Mix well. Sift the flours, baking powder, baking soda, and salt. Add orange peel.

Add flour mixture alternately with the orange juice to the creamed mixture. Beat lightly and stir in the nuts.

Pour into greased 8″ × 5″ loaf pan or into smaller pans and bake in preheated 350° oven until the bread pulls away from the sides of pans and is lightly browned, approximately 45 minutes or less for smaller pans.

The bread is better if ripened overnight before serving.

PUMPKIN BREAD

One of the best of the sweet breads. The texture of this rivals any bread made with gluten flour. It stays moist and doesn't need heating to taste good. The spices, pumpkin, and pecans give it a flavor reminiscent of pumpkin pie. But don't save this just for Thanksgiving. It is good anytime.

1 cup GF flour mix	2 eggs
1/2 teaspoon baking soda	2/3 cup canned pumpkin
1 teaspoon baking powder	1/4 cup mayonnaise
1/4 cup sugar	2 tablespoons chopped
1/2 teaspoon salt	pecans, or 2 tablespoons
1 1/2 teaspoons pumpkin	chopped dates or raisins
pie spice	

Combine flour, baking soda, baking powder, sugar, salt, and spice in mixing bowl. In another bowl, beat eggs, then add pumpkin and mayonnaise. Pour this into flour mixture. Stir all together well. Add pecans or dried fruit and pour into a greased 4″ × 8″ loaf pan or two small ones (5″ × 2 1/2″). Bake the larger pan for 1 hour in preheated 350° oven or the smaller ones for about 45 to 50 minutes.

LENTIL SESAME BREAD

Don't be put off by the lentils in this bread. No one will ever guess what makes this dark, fine-textured loaf so tasty. It is good with cream cheese or just sliced and buttered for a snack.

This is a variation of a recipe developed by Elaine Hartsook for the Gluten Intolerance Group.

3/4 cup lentils	1 teaspoon baking soda
1/2 cup (1 stick)	1/2 teaspoon salt
margarine, melted	1/2 teaspoon curry powder
1/2 cup sugar	1 1/2 teaspoons baking
3 eggs	powder
1 cup rice flour	2 tablespoons sesame seeds
1/2 cup potato flour	

Wash lentils and put in 1¹/₂- to 2-quart pan. Add 3 cups water and bring to boil over high heat. Cover and simmer until lentils are tender, about 40 minutes, unless the package says otherwise. Drain and cool.

In a large bowl, mix together margarine, sugar, and eggs. Stir in lentils. Mix together flours, baking soda, salt, curry powder, baking powder, and sesame seeds. Stir into lentil mixture until well combined.

Pour into a 5″ × 9″ loaf pan or 3 small 2¹/₂″ × 5″ pans that have been greased and floured. Bake in oven preheated to 350° until loaf just begins to pull from sides of pan and top is tinged brown, about 1 hour for large loaf and about 40 minutes for small. Cool 10 minutes before removing from pan.

This freezes well for storage. Slice before freezing.

SMALL BREADS

Most of the breads at the beginning of this chapter were planned for loaf-sized pans. The ones in this section are what my mother called the "small breads," those stirred up specifically to be made in smaller sizes such as muffins, cornbreads, and popovers. They are mostly quick breads easily whipped up for a meal and, although usually served hot from the oven or pan, several of them make excellent substitutes for bread in sandwiches. The corn muffins are great with cheese and ham; the popovers especially good in a lunch box with fillings of chicken or tuna fish blended with mayonnaise.

Many of these recipes call for a mix of rice, potato starch, and tapioca flours. The formula for this can be found on page 24.

QUICK AND EASY MUFFINS

These are a standby for me when I run out of bread. They take only one pan to mix and taste good both hot and cold. These come out best when mixed by hand with a mixing spoon.

$1/4$ cup sugar	$1/4$ teaspoon salt
2 tablespoons shortening	2 teaspoons baking powder
2 eggs	$1/2$ cup milk or nondairy
1 cup GF flour mix or all	liquid
rice flour	$1/4$ teaspoon vanilla

In the mixing bowl, cream together sugar and shortening. Then beat in the eggs.

Sift together the flour, salt, and baking powder and add to the egg mixture alternately with the milk. Don't overbeat. Stir in the vanilla.

Pour into greased muffin cups. Bake in preheated 350° oven for about 20 minutes. *Makes about 8 muffins.*

BLUEBERRY OR
CRANBERRY MUFFINS

Follow the recipe for Quick and Easy Muffins and add 1 to 1 $1/2$ tablespoons of blueberries or cranberries, fresh or frozen. (I keep these in a bag in the freezer and break apart what I need as I use them. It doesn't hurt the muffins to put them in still frozen.)

RICE BRAN MUFFINS

This is a variation on Quick and Easy Muffins but the bran changes the taste. I often add raisins to this batter.

1/4 cup brown sugar
2 tablespoons shortening
2 eggs
2/3 cup brown rice flour
1 tablespoon tapioca flour
2 tablespoons potato
starch flour

2 teaspoons baking powder
1/2 teaspoon salt
3/4 cup milk or nondairy
liquid
1/2 cup rice bran
Optional: 1/4 cup raisins

Cream together the sugar and shortening. Add the eggs, beating after each one.

Sift the flours together with the baking powder and salt. Add to the egg mixture alternately with the milk. Stir in rice bran last, then raisins if using.

Bake in greased muffin tins in preheated 350° oven for 20 to 25 minutes. *Makes approximately 8 muffins.*

KASHA (BUCKWHEAT) MUFFINS

This nutty-tasting variation of the bran muffin is an excellent change. Buckwheat supposedly* contains no gluten, so celiacs should be able to eat this kasha form, thus getting more fiber into their diets.

1/3 cup brown sugar
2 tablespoons shortening
2 eggs
2/3 cup brown rice flour
1 tablespoon tapioca flour
2 tablespoons potato
starch flour

2 teaspoons baking powder
3/4 cup milk
1/2 cup kasha (roasted
buckwheat kernels)
1 teaspoon grated orange
peel

Cream together the sugar and shortening. Add the eggs, beating after each one.

Sift the flours together with the baking powder and add to the egg

*Despite its name, buckwheat is not a member of the wheat family; botanically speaking, it is a fruit, says the National Buckwheat Institute.

mixture alternately with the milk. Stir in buckwheat kernels and grated orange peel last.

Bake in greased muffin tins in preheated 350° oven for 20 to 25 minutes. *Makes approximately 8 muffins.*

ZUCCHINI MUFFINS

These spicy, tender muffins stay fresh-tasting and moist for several days because of the zucchini in the recipe. They are my favorite during the zucchini season.

$1/3$ cup sugar	$1/2$ teaspoon baking soda
2 eggs	$1/4$ teaspoon cinnamon
3 tablespoons vegetable oil	$1/4$ teaspoon nutmeg
1 cup GF flour mixture	1 cup grated zucchini
1 teaspoon baking powder	$1/4$ cup raisins
$3/4$ teaspoon salt	$1/4$ cup chopped walnuts

Beat together the sugar, eggs, and oil.

Combine the flour, baking powder, salt, baking soda, cinnamon, and nutmeg. Stir these into the sugar mixture. The batter will seem dry. Stir in the zucchini, raisins, and nuts.

Grease muffin tins and spoon in batter to two-thirds full. Bake in preheated 400° oven for 20 minutes. *Makes 10 to 12 muffins.*

SPICY CARROT MUFFINS

This is another muffin that stays moist. It's so good it's almost dessert.

$1 1/2$ cups GF flour mix	1 cup shredded carrots
$1/2$ cup rice bran	$2/3$ cup orange juice
1 teaspoon cinnamon	$1/3$ cup raisins
$3/4$ teaspoon baking soda	$1/4$ cup vegetable oil
2 teaspoons baking powder	$1/4$ cup brown sugar
$1/4$ teaspoon nutmeg	2 eggs

In a large bowl, combine flour, bran, cinnamon, baking soda, baking powder, and nutmeg. Mix well.

Combine carrots, orange juice, raisins, oil, brown sugar, and eggs and add to dry mixture, mixing until dry ingredients are moistened.

Grease 10 medium muffin cups or line them with paper liners. Fill about two-thirds full of batter. Let stand 5 minutes.

Bake in a preheated 425° oven for 20 to 25 minutes.

BUTTERMILK BISCUITS

Biscuits are more difficult to make with a rice flour base, since the cook does not usually have egg for leavening. But these (with the one egg added) have proved very good. They may be used as a bread substitute or as a base for creamed foods or berry shortcake.

1 tablespoon sugar	2 teaspoons baking powder
3 tablespoons shortening	1/2 teaspoon baking soda
1 egg	1/2 teaspoon salt
1/2 cup rice flour	1/3 cup buttermilk
1/3 cup potato starch flour	

Mix the sugar, shortening, and egg. Sift the dry ingredients together and add them to the sugar mixture alternately with the buttermilk.

Pat out the mixture onto rice-floured wax paper and cut into round biscuit shapes. Or make drop biscuits by dropping the batter by tablespoonfuls onto a greased baking sheet.

Bake on a greased baking sheet in a preheated 400° oven for 12 to 15 minutes. *Makes eight 2 1/2-inch biscuits.*

POPOVERS

Easy to make and impressive. This batter is very forgiving and always turns out.

1 cup water	²/₃ cup rice flour
¹/₂ cup shortening	¹/₂ teaspoon salt
¹/₃ cup potato starch flour*	4 eggs

Combine water and shortening in large saucepan. Bring to rapid boil. Remove from stove. Add flours and salt all at once. Stir until mixture forms a ball that leaves the sides of pan. Cool slightly. Add unbeaten eggs one at a time, beating well with electric mixer after each egg is added.

Drop by tablespoons into greased muffin tins to form a goose-egg-sized mound. Bake 20 minutes in preheated 450° oven, then reduce heat and bake 20 minutes at 350°. *Makes about 15 popovers.*

*You may use all rice flour, but the resulting texture will be grainier.

SUGAR-FREE
WHITE CORN MUFFINS

I have included several cornbreads but these are, perhaps, my favorites, for they come out moist and tasting a bit like hominy grits.

2 cups white cornmeal	2 tablespoons butter or margarine, melted
1¹/₂ teaspoons salt	1 cup cold milk or nondairy liquid
2 cups boiling water	4 teaspoons baking powder
2 eggs	

In a large bowl, mix together the cornmeal and salt. Gradually stir in the boiling water. Beat with spoon until smooth.

Beat the eggs and stir these, the melted butter, and the milk into the flour mixture. Finally stir in the baking powder.

Pour into well-greased muffin cups. Bake in preheated 425° oven for 25 to 30 minutes. *Makes about 16 muffins.*

YELLOW CORN MUFFINS

For an entirely different taste and texture from the preceding muffins, try these dry and fluffy ones.

1 cup yellow cornmeal	1 teaspoon salt
1 cup corn flour	2 eggs, beaten
1/4 cup sugar	1 cup buttermilk
2 teaspoons baking powder	2 tablespoons shortening,
1 teaspoon baking soda	melted

Sift the dry ingredients together into mixing bowl. Stir in the beaten eggs, buttermilk, and melted shortening.

Pour into greased muffin cups. Bake in preheated 400° oven for about 25 minutes. *Makes about 12 muffins.*

ORANGE CORNBREAD

The use of fresh grated orange rind and of corn flour instead of cornmeal makes this different in both texture and taste. This may be eaten hot from the oven as a bread, but try it other ways. It makes a great dressing for your Thanksgiving turkey (see page 210) and is perfect for stuffed pork chops or as a dressing beside a pork roast.

2 cups corn flour	3 eggs, beaten
2 tablespoons sugar	1/3 cup vegetable oil
4 teaspoons baking powder	2 teaspoons grated orange
1/2 teaspoon salt	peel
1 cup milk	

In mixing bowl, combine corn flour, sugar, baking powder, and salt. Stir in milk, eggs, oil, and orange peel until smooth. Do not overbeat.

Pour into a greased 9″ × 9″ × 2″ baking pan. Bake in preheated 400° oven for 20 to 25 minutes. *Serves 6 to 8 as a cornbread or stuffs a 12- to 14-pound turkey.*

COOKIES

Cookies are probably the easiest baked item to make from gluten-free flours, and the results are almost always satisfying.

In the following pages you'll find a wide range of cookies that have turned out successfully in my kitchen. They range from the Chewy Fruit Bars that remind you of Christmas fruitcake to Butterscotch Chip Dreams you will have to hide from the rest of the family to have any for the celiac. There's even one nonbake recipe easy enough for children to make.

Some of these travel better than others. Those I carry on trips to have a sweet when others have a gluten-filled dessert.

Each recipe calls for a different combination of flours. Many use a combination of rice and soy, while others call for the GF flour mixture suggested earlier. For your convenience, here's the three-part formula again:

> 2 parts white rice flour
> 2/3 part potato starch flour
> 1/3 part tapioca flour

DROP COOKIES

BUTTERSCOTCH BITES

An easy-to-make drop cookie that tastes great. These keep well in the cookie jar at home but don't travel as well as some of the other cookies, since they are moist and chewy and tend to stick together when bumped around.

1/2 cup (1 stick) butter or margarine
1 cup dark brown sugar
1 egg

1/2 cup rice flour
1/2 cup soy flour
1/2 cup chopped pecans

Beat butter or margarine and sugar together until creamy. Beat in egg, then flours. Add nuts last.

Drop by teaspoonfuls onto ungreased cookie sheets. Bake in preheated 375° oven for 10 to 12 minutes. Remove immediately from baking sheet and let cool on wax paper. Store loosely covered. *Makes approximately 3 dozen cookies.*

BUTTERSCOTCH CHIP DREAMS

A rich, moist cookie that will surprise your gluten-eating friends. This cookie keeps well for the lunch box. I like them made with butterscotch chips, but you may substitute chocolate chips or peanut butter chips.

1 cup (2 sticks) butter or margarine
1 cup brown sugar
2 eggs
1 teaspoon vanilla
2 cups soy flour

1/4 cup rice flour
1 teaspoon baking soda
1/2 teaspoon salt
One 12-ounce package butterscotch chips

In a large bowl, beat with an electric mixer the butter or margarine, brown sugar, eggs, and vanilla. Combine the flours, baking soda, and salt and add to the creamed mixture. Then stir in the chips.

Drop by teaspoonfuls onto ungreased cookie sheets. Bake in preheated 350° oven for approximately 10 minutes. *Makes approximately 3 dozen cookies.*

PEANUT BUTTER DROPS

No, I didn't forget the flour in this one. The recipe doesn't call for any. Since this is a cookie that keeps and travels well, it's great for that quick energy snack on trips.

2 eggs
1 cup chunky peanut butter
1 cup sugar

Beat the eggs. Stir in the peanut butter and sugar.

Drop by small spoonfuls on ungreased cookie sheets. Bake in preheated 350° oven for 10 to 12 minutes. *Makes approximately 2½ dozen 2-inch cookies.*

FORGOTTEN DREAMS

A meringue cookie that tastes more like candy than cookie. Easy to make. Can be made late at night and left in the oven overnight.

2 egg whites
1/8 teaspoon salt
1/2 teaspoon cream of
   tartar

1/2 cup sugar
1/2 teaspoon vanilla
6 ounces butterscotch
   chips

With electric beater, beat egg whites until foamy. Add salt and cream of tartar. Beat until whites form stiff peaks.

Add sugar gradually, while beating. Beat in vanilla. Fold in the butterscotch chips (or peanut butter chips if you prefer). Drop by teaspoonfuls on greased cookie sheets. Put in oven that has been preheated to 350°. *Turn oven off* and forget for 2 hours or more. *Makes about 60 small cookies.*

COCONUT MACAROONS

Although we can sometimes find GF macaroons on the cookie shelf in the supermarket, these are far tastier than any store-bought cookies, and contain no flour.

1/2 teaspoon salt	1 teaspoon vanilla
4 egg whites	2 cups sweetened shredded
1 1/4 cups fine granulated	coconut
sugar	

Add salt to egg whites and beat with electric mixer until stiff but not dry. Add sugar slowly, beating until granules are dissolved. Mix in lightly the vanilla and coconut. Drop by teaspoonfuls onto ungreased brown paper on cookie sheets.

Bake in preheated 350° oven for about 20 minutes. Slip paper onto wet table or board and let stand for 1 minute. Loosen cookies and remove to wire racks. *Makes approximately 2 1/2 dozen macaroons.*

PECAN BITES

Another cookie more like candy than cookie. Like the preceding recipe, it contains no flour.

3 egg whites	1/4 teaspoon salt
3 cups light brown sugar	1 teaspoon vanilla
3 cups chopped pecans	

Beat the egg whites to soft peaks. Stir in the rest of the ingredients. Drop by scant tablespoonfuls onto greased cookie sheets. Bake in preheated 300° oven for about 20 minutes. *Makes approximately 6 dozen cookies.*

CARROT RAISIN DROP COOKIES

These tender cookies are studded with raisins and nuts. The carrots give moistness, the rice polish (or cereal) adds fiber. The cookies keep well— if you hide them away.

1 cup GF flour mix	1/2 cup (1 stick) butter or
1/2 cup soy flour	margarine
1 rounded teaspoon baking	3 large eggs
soda	1 cup corn syrup
2 teaspoons pumpkin pie	2 cups grated carrots
spice	1 cup raisins
1 cup rice polish*	1/2 cup chopped walnuts

In a bowl, mix together flours, baking soda, spice, and rice polish.

In another bowl, beat butter, eggs, and Karo with an electric mixer until blended. Mix in the carrots. Add the flour mixture. Stir until mixed, then beat until blended. Stir in raisins and nuts.

Spoon dough in tablespoon-sized mounds 2 inches apart on greased baking sheets. Bake in preheated 350° oven until cookies feel firm when touched, 12 to 14 minutes. Remove from pans and cool. *Makes about 4 dozen cookies.*

*You may replace rice polish with 1 1/2 cups crushed gluten-free cereal. Or try crushed Vita Fiber, a processed rice polish that has been made into flakes.

BAR COOKIES

NO-BAKE
PEANUT BUTTER BARS

Easy enough for even children to make, but a satisfying, chewy treat for the whole family.

6 cups gluten-free puffed
  or crisped rice cereal
1 cup raisins
1 cup dark corn syrup

1 cup chunky peanut
  butter
1 cup sugar

In a large bowl, mix the rice cereal and raisins together. Set aside while you heat the syrup, peanut butter, and sugar in a saucepan over low heat until it bubbles.

Pour the hot syrup over the rice cereal and raisins and blend together. Press the mixture into a buttered 9″ × 13″ pan. Cut into squares when cool. *Makes 2 dozen 2- × -2-inch cookies.*

BUTTERSCOTCH BROWNIES

If you're hungry for the taste of cakelike brownies, these are my first choice, for they are easy to make and turn out moist and flavorful. They also will completely satisfy those who can eat gluten.

1/2 cup (1 stick)
  margarine*
2 cups firmly packed
  brown sugar
1 teaspoon vanilla
3 eggs

1 cup rice flour
1/2 cup soy flour
2 teaspoons baking
  powder
1/2 teaspoon salt
1 cup finely chopped nuts

*For an even more tender bar, try Butter Flavor Crisco.

Cream margarine with the brown sugar. Add vanilla and eggs and beat with electric mixer until light. Combine the flours, baking powder, and salt. Add to egg mixture. Mix at low speed until blended. Stir in the nuts.

Spread the mixture evenly in a greased 9″ × 13″ pan. Bake in preheated 350° oven for 25 to 30 minutes or until top is light brown. Cool 10 to 15 minutes before cutting into bars. *Makes 2 dozen bars.*

CHUNKY
CHOCOLATE SQUARES

For all chocolate lovers. A no-fuss cookie, rich with nuts and chocolate.

1 1/4 cups rice flour	3/4 cup corn syrup
1 1/4 cups soy flour	2 eggs
1 1/2 teaspoons baking soda	1 teaspoon vanilla
1/2 teaspoon salt	One 8-ounce package
3/4 cup (1 1/2 sticks)	semisweet chocolate
margarine or butter	squares
1 cup brown sugar	1 cup chopped nuts

In a small bowl, combine the rice and soy flours, baking soda, and salt; set aside. In a mixing bowl, beat butter and sugar with mixer at medium until fluffy. Slowly beat in the corn syrup, then eggs and vanilla. Beat in the prepared flour mixture until blended. Cut the chocolate squares into 1/2-inch chunks. Stir in the nuts and half the chocolate chunks.

Spread the batter evenly in an ungreased 15 1/2″ × 10 1/2″ jelly roll pan or a cookie sheet with raised sides. Sprinkle the remaining chocolate on top. Bake in preheated 350° oven for 30 minutes or until lightly browned. Cool in pan before cutting into 2-inch squares. *Makes 3 dozen cookies.*

HELLO DOLLYS

A rich candylike bar cookie with a combination of flavors that melt in your mouth. Extra easy to make.

1/2 cup (1 stick) margarine
1 cup crushed GF cereal*
1 cup shredded sweetened
coconut
6 ounces (1/2 package)
chocolate chips

6 ounces (1/2 package)
butterscotch chips
1 can sweetened condensed
milk
1 cup chopped nuts

In a 9″ × 13″ pan, melt the margarine. Then add in layers the rest of the ingredients in the order listed. Bake 30 minutes in preheated 325° oven. When cool, cut in 1- to 1 1/2-inch squares. *Makes 4 1/2 to 5 dozen cookies.*

*Good also with dried GF bread crumbs with 1 added tablespoon of sugar. Absolutely wonderful with Ginger-Almond cookie crumbs.

ORANGE-SLICE BARS

This recipe, clipped from a magazine over twenty-five years ago, became a family Christmas favorite. Even converted to the rice-soy flour mixture, it remains one. This cookie keeps and travels well.

1 pound candy orange
slices
1 1/2 cups rice flour
1/2 cup soy flour
1/2 teaspoon salt

3 cups light brown
sugar
4 eggs, slightly beaten
1 cup chopped nuts
1 teaspoon vanilla

Cut orange slices into small pieces with scissors dipped in cold water (or in sugar). Add to flours and salt. Add remaining ingredients and mix well. Spread in greased 9″ × 13″ pan or two 8″ × 8″ pans. Bake in preheated 350° oven for about 45 minutes. Cool in pan. Cut into 1-×-2-inch bars. *Makes 3 to 4 dozen bars.*

FIG BARS

A rich, fruit-filled bar high in fiber and flavor. The filling can be changed to apricot, pineapple, prune, or date.

3/4 cup dried figs	1 1/2 cups brown sugar
3/4 cup raisins	1 1/2 cups (3 sticks) butter
1 1/2 cups orange juice	or margarine
2 cups rice flour	1 cup rice bran
1/2 cup soy flour	1 cup chopped walnuts
1 teaspoon xanthan gum	2 eggs, beaten
1/2 teaspoon salt	

Cut the figs into small pieces and combine with the raisins and orange juice in a small saucepan. Bring to a boil, reduce heat, and simmer for 20 minutes, stirring occasionally, until the mixture is thickened. Let cool a bit and, if it isn't smooth, place in blender and purée.

In a mixing bowl, combine the flours, xanthan gum, salt, and brown sugar. Cut in the butter until the mixture is crumbly. Stir in the bran, walnuts, and beaten eggs. Don't worry if the mixture seems to be crumbly. Just press half into the bottom of a 9″ × 13″ baking pan and spread the fruit mixture over this. Top with the second half of the dough, patting it smooth. The dough will blend together as it bakes. Bake in preheated 350° oven for 45 minutes.

Let cool completely in the pan before cutting into 1-inch squares. *Makes about 8 1/2 dozen small bars.*

CHEWY FRUIT BARS

This moist, chewy bar keeps and travels well. It has a light fruitcake flavor so is especially tasty for a Christmas cookie.

10 ounces fruit cake mix
1/2 cup fruit juice (orange, apple, or cranberry)
1 teaspoon grated orange peel
2 eggs
1/2 cup shortening

1 1/3 cups brown sugar
3/4 cup rice flour
3/4 cup soy flour
1 teaspoon baking powder
1 teaspoon cinnamon
1/2 teaspoon salt

In a small bowl, combine the fruit cake mix, fruit juice, and grated orange peel. Set aside.

In mixing bowl, beat together the eggs, shortening, and brown sugar. Then combine the flours, baking powder, cinnamon, and salt and add to the egg-shortening mixture. Stir in the fruit mix.

Spread the dough in a greased and rice-floured 9″ × 13″ pan or on a cookie sheet with raised sides and bake 25 to 30 minutes in preheated 350° oven. Let cool slightly and cut into 2-inch squares or diamond shapes by marking diagonally across pan in both directions. *Makes 30 bars.*

SHAPED COOKIES

GINGERSNAPS

A spicy, cholesterol-free, high-fiber taste treat. For an even higher fiber cookie, replace 1/4 cup of the flour with rice bran or with crushed Vita Fiber.

1 1/2 cups brown rice flour   1/4 teaspoon salt
1 teaspoon powdered   1/2 cup honey
  ginger   3 tablespoons molasses
1 teaspoon cinnamon

In a small mixing bowl, mix together the flour, spices, and salt. Add the honey and molasses and stir together. This will make a stiff dough. Work it until it forms a ball.

Dampen your hands and pinch off small sections to roll into 3/4-inch balls. Place these 3 inches apart on a greased cookie sheet. After making all the dough into balls, press each flat (1/4 inch thick) with the bottom of a wet glass dipped in granulated sugar.

Bake in preheated 350° oven for 12 to 15 minutes. Do not leave in oven longer than 15 minutes. These brown only slightly. Remove from cookie sheet immediately. *Makes 2 dozen cookies 1 1/2 inches in diameter.*

OLD-FASHIONED
SUGAR COOKIES

No cookbook would be complete without at least one sugar cookie recipe. But, unlike some of the richer cookies where egg and soy replaced the stretch factor of the missing gluten, the sugar cookie took a lot of experimentation. This one is easy to handle and can be cut into intricate shapes with the cookie cutter. Decorate by sprinkling with colored sugar before baking or with frosting after baking.

1 1/2 cups sugar   1 1/2 cups potato starch
1 cup Butter Flavor   flour
  Crisco   2/3 cup cornstarch
4 egg yolks   2/3 cup tapioca flour
1 teaspoon dried orange   2 teaspoons baking powder
  peel or vanilla   1 teaspoon salt

In a large mixing bowl, blend the sugar and shortening. Add egg yolks and flavoring. Mix flours, baking powder, and salt together and add to the first mixture. This will seem crumbly, but work the dough with your hands until you can form balls.

Roll out dough on wax paper to about 1/8 inch thick. Cut into desired shapes and transfer to greased cookie sheets. Bake in preheated 375° oven for 8 to 10 minutes. When cool, frost if desired. *Makes 6 dozen 2-inch cookies.*

NOTE: Don't be afraid to handle this dough. It doesn't toughen with handling.

PRALINES

A firm, flat cookie with a flavor reminiscent of the New Orleans candy from which it gets its name. This is another good traveler and keeper, for the flavor seems to improve with age.

1/2 cup (1 stick) butter or margarine	2 eggs
1 1/2 cups dark brown sugar	3/4 cup rice flour
	3/4 cup soy flour
	1/2 cup chopped pecans

In a mixing bowl, beat butter and sugar together until creamy; beat in eggs, then flours. Add nuts. Chill 1 hour.

Roll pieces of dough into 1-inch balls; place on greased baking sheets 3 inches apart. Moisten bottom of glass tumbler; press balls to flatten to 1/8-inch thickness. Bake in preheated 375° oven 10 to 12 minutes or until lightly browned. Remove immediately from baking sheets and cool. *Makes 3 dozen cookies.*

REFRIGERATOR ROLL

A basic dough to which you can add your choice of nuts, raisins, coconut, or chocolate and freeze to pull out and bake when you feel like cookies.

1/2 cup (1 stick) butter or margarine
1 1/2 cups white or brown sugar
1 egg
3/4 cup rice flour

3/4 cup soy flour
Nuts, raisins, sweetened or unsweetened coconut, chopped candied cherries or citron, or chocolate, as desired

Cream the butter and sugar. Beat in the egg, then the flours. The dough will be similar to soft pastry. Add any of the following: 1/2 to 1 cup chopped nuts, 1/2 cup chopped raisins, 1/2 to 3/4 cup shredded coconut, chopped candied cherries or citron, 1 or 2 squares melted chocolate.

For a marbled look to the chocolate, use less of the melted chocolate and just blend until you achieve a marbled texture. For a butterscotch flavor, use dark brown sugar. You may separate the dough and make two different kinds of cookies from the one batch.

Roll the dough in a long roll about 1 1/2 inches in diameter and about 12 inches long, or into 2 shorter rolls, each about 6 inches long. Wrap in plastic and refrigerate 1 hour before slicing about 1/6 inch thick. Bake on greased cookie sheets in preheated 375° oven for 10 to 12 minutes. *Makes 6 dozen cookies.*

JAM-FILLED CRUNCHIES

A rich, tasty cookie for special treats. The surprise is in the crunch. These are tender and do not travel well.

1 cup (2 sticks) butter or margarine
2/3 cup sugar
1 teaspoon vanilla
1 egg
1 1/2 cups rice flour

1/2 cup soy flour
3/4 cup crushed potato chips
1/2 cup chopped pecans
1/4 cup raspberry or apricot jam

Beat butter, all but 2 tablespoons of sugar, and vanilla in a mixing bowl until fluffy. Stir in the egg, then flours, potato chips, and pecans. Mix until blended.

Roll dough into 1 1/4-inch balls. Place on ungreased cookie sheets and flatten each ball with the back of a teaspoon dipped in the remaining sugar. Dot each cookie center with 1/4 teaspoon jam.

Bake in preheated 350° oven for 16 to 18 minutes or until lightly browned. These should be stored airtight for a couple of days or frozen. *Makes 3 1/2 dozen cookies.*

GINGER-ALMOND STICKS

A crisp, spicy stick to go with your coffee, milk, or wine. This very different cookie is baked twice, but after you've tasted one you'll agree they're well worth the extra trouble. (The cookies will crumble less if you use the xanthan gum.)

1 cup slivered almonds	1 tablespoon baking
3/4 cup sugar	powder
1/2 cup (1 stick) butter or	1 tablespoon cinnamon
margarine	1 teaspoon nutmeg
1/2 cup molasses	1/2 teaspoon cloves
1/4 cup grated fresh ginger	1/2 teaspoon allspice
4 eggs	Optional: 1 teaspoon
3 cups GF flour mix	xanthan gum

Place almonds in an 8" square pan and bake in preheated 350° oven until lightly toasted, 10 to 15 minutes. Let cool and then chop coarsely and set aside.

In a large mixing bowl, beat sugar, butter, molasses, and ginger with an electric mixer until smooth. Add the eggs, one at a time, beating after each addition. Mix together the flour, baking powder, cinnamon, nutmeg, cloves, allspice, almonds, and xanthan gum if used. Add to the egg mixture, stirring to blend.

Grease 2 cookie sheets. Using your hands, pat the dough into 4 flat loaves on the sheets. Each loaf should be about $^1/_2$ inch thick, 2 inches wide, and the length of the baking sheet. (I use plastic wrap to cover my hands as I pat the dough into shape.) Bake in preheated 350° oven about 25 minutes, reversing the position of the cookie sheets in the oven halfway through the baking. Done, the loaves should be browned at the edges and springy to touch.

Let loaves stand on the cookie sheets until cool to touch, then cut into $^1/_2$-inch-thick diagonal slices across the loaves. Arrange the slices on their sides on the baking sheets and return to the oven to bake again until the cookies are brown and crisp, 15 to 18 minutes. Again, reverse the position of the baking sheets halfway through baking.

Let sticks cool to serve or store airtight up to 1 month, or freeze them. *Makes about 4 dozen sticks.*

NOTE: Be sure to save any broken sticks and all the crumbs. On page 92 there's a recipe for using the crumbs and leftovers for a pastry crust. A gourmet treat!

DATE ROLL-UPS

This unusual cookie made of pastry wrapped around dates or nuts gives variety to a plate of mixed goodies. The tender cream cheese crust lends a different taste for the palate.

One 8-ounce package
   cream cheese
1 cup (2 sticks) butter or
   margarine
1 $^1/_2$ cups rice flour
$^1/_4$ cup tapioca flour

$^1/_4$ cup cornstarch
1 teaspoon salt
One 12-ounce package
   pitted dates, or 1 cup
   walnut halves

Soften the cream cheese and cream with the butter or margarine. Thoroughly blend the flours, cornstarch, and salt; add to the creamed mixture. This should resemble soft pie dough. Refrigerate 1 hour or until firm.

Remove dough from refrigerator and work into 2 balls. Roll them out, one at a time, on a board sprinkled with powdered sugar and cut with a pastry wheel into 1- × -4-inch oblongs. Roll these around the dates or walnuts.

Tuck the flap sides down and bake on cookie sheets in preheated 375° oven for 15 or 20 minutes. *Makes approximately 6 dozen pastries.*

CAKES

Some of today's homemakers are so used to cake mixes or picking up a cake in a bakery that starting from scratch may seem more effort than it is worth, but for anyone who cannot tolerate gluten, this is the only way to have a cake and eat it, too.

The recipes in this section have been selected because, in most instances, they are the easiest and the tastiest using our flours. They cover a wide range, from a simple white cake through the fruit and carrot cakes. For these cakes, I use different combinations of white rice flour, potato starch flour, tapioca flour, and soy flour.

For many of them I use my standard gluten-free flour mix, which I keep on hand at all times. To remind you, the formula is:

2 parts white rice flour
$2/3$ part potato starch flour
$1/3$ part tapioca flour

For heavier or moister cakes, I replace the tapioca with soy flour, giving the cakes a better texture and richer flavor. The recipes for these cakes will have their formulas listed in the ingredients, for each seems to need a different amount of soy. If you can't tolerate soy, you can still use the GF flour mixture above in these cakes.

LEMON SHEET CAKE

Plain white cakes often turn out dry and crumbly using gluten-free flours. I almost despaired of baking a successful white cake until I developed this recipe, which makes a fine-textured, moist cake. It may be frosted, cut into shapes and made into petit fours, or used as a shortcake with berries. This is also a quick cake to mix, using only the one bowl.

4 large eggs	2 tablespoons lemon
1 cup sugar	juice
1 teaspoon vanilla	3/4 cup GF flour mix
1/4 cup vegetable oil	Optional: 1/2 teaspoon
1 tablespoon grated lemon	xanthan gum
peel	

Beat eggs and sugar together with electric mixer at high speed for approximately 5 minutes. Add vanilla, oil, lemon peel, lemon juice, and flour sifted with xanthan gum. (Xanthan gum will make texture firmer and less crumbly.) Beat until smooth.

Pour batter into greased and rice-flour-dusted 7″ × 11″ baking pan. Bake in preheated 375° oven for 25 to 35 minutes, or until cake begins to pull from sides of pan and top feels set when touched lightly. *Makes 6 to 8 servings.*

For variation, add 1/2 cup chopped nuts and 1/2 cup raisins and serve as a coffee cake.

PINEAPPLE OR PEACH UPSIDE-DOWN CAKE

This variation of the preceding cake is an old family favorite. The addition of the fruit topping saves making a frosting and keeps the cake more moist. This is especially tasty served hot from the oven.

    1 recipe Lemon Sheet Cake, page 68
    1/3 cup (2/3 stick) butter or margarine
    1/2 cup brown sugar
    One 28-ounce can peach halves or pineapple slices, drained

Prepare cake batter.

Instead of greasing the 7″ × 11″ cake pan, use a combination of the butter and brown sugar melted together in the pan. Then arrange the pineapple or peach halves, cut sides down, in the sugar mixture. Carefully spoon on the batter.

Bake in preheated 375° oven for 25 to 35 minutes. Serve in squares, fruit side up, topped with whipped cream. *Makes 6 to 8 servings.*

CLASSIC SPONGE CAKE

A fine-textured, springy cake with delicate flavor that is excellent eaten plain or with fruit. Or it can be glazed by drizzling on a thin mixture of butter, powdered sugar, and lemon juice. It keeps well.

1/2 cup rice flour	7 eggs, separated
1/2 cup tapioca flour	1 teaspoon grated lemon
3/4 teaspoon baking	peel
powder	3/4 cup sugar
1/4 teaspoon salt	1 teaspoon cream of tartar

Sift together the flours, baking powder, and salt. Set aside.

Separate the eggs, placing the yolks in a 1 1/2-quart bowl and the whites in a large mixing bowl. With mixer, whip the yolks on high speed for 3 to 5 minutes. Add the lemon peel and continue to whip until thick and pale yellow.

With clean beaters, whip the whites for a minute. Add 1 tablespoon sugar and the cream of tartar and continue whipping for 4 to 5 minutes or until the whites are glossy and stiff. Remove mixer.

Pour the yolks onto the whites and gently fold together. Sprinkle about 1/3 of the remaining sugar over surface and fold to incorporate. Add the rest in two more foldings. In the same way, in three additions, add the flour mixture, folding each time until just incorporated.

Pour the batter into an ungreased 9″ tube pan. Bake in preheated 300° oven for about 50 to 60 minutes, or until the cake springs back when pressed with finger.

To cool, turn the pan upside down and let stand for 2 hours before removing cake. (If your tube pan doesn't have raised "feet" around the rim, hang it by its tube over a soda bottle.)

ORANGE CHIFFON CAKE

A fine, spongy cake that lasts—unless you let nonceliacs taste it. This is one of my favorite "company" cakes, for it doesn't taste grainy or dry out as fast as some nongluten baked products do. I drizzle this lightly with a frosting of powdered sugar, a bit of butter, and some orange juice, which I mix thin enough to pour easily. You might prefer to use a cream cheese frosting (page 85). The cake can also be served with whipped cream or an orange sauce, or used for strawberry shortcake.

If you wish, you may substitute 2 cups sifted GF flour mix for the rice flour and potato starch flour.

1 1/3 cups rice flour	1/2 cup vegetable oil
2/3 cup potato starch flour	7 eggs, separated
1 1/2 cups sugar	3/4 cup orange juice
1 tablespoon baking powder	2 teaspoons grated orange rind
1 teaspoon salt	1/2 teaspoon cream of tartar

Sift together into a mixing bowl the flours, sugar, baking powder, and salt. Make a well in the dry ingredients and add in order: oil, unbeaten egg yolks, orange juice, and rind. Beat together with a spoon until smooth.

In a large bowl, beat with electric mixer the egg whites and cream of tartar until they form very stiff peaks. Pour the egg yolk mixture gradually over the whipped whites, gently folding with a rubber scraper until just blended.

Pour batter into a large ungreased tube pan or a 9″ × 13″ oblong pan. Bake tube pan in preheated 325° oven for 55 minutes, then raise temperature to 350° for 10 to 15 minutes. Bake oblong pan in preheated 350° oven for 45 to 50 minutes.

SURPRISE CHOCOLATE CAKE

A moist, tasty chocolate cake sure to win raves at any party. This recipe is adapted from one developed by Elaine Hartsook for the Gluten Intolerance Group. The secret is the unusual ingredient, lentil purée, but don't tell anyone. They'll never guess.

2/3 cup dry lentils	2 squares baking chocolate
2 cups boiling water	2 cups GF flour mix
1 1/2 cups sugar	1 1/2 teaspoons baking soda
1 cup vegetable oil	2 teaspoons baking powder
4 large eggs	1/2 teaspoon salt
1 teaspoon vanilla	

Rinse and drain lentils and combine in saucepan with the boiling water. Bring to a boil, cover, and let simmer 40 minutes. Drain, reserving liquid. Purée the lentils and 1/4 cup of reserved liquid in blender or food processor. You will need 1 3/4 cups of purée for the recipe.

In bowl of your mixer, combine sugar, oil, and eggs. Beat well. Add vanilla and 1 3/4 cups lentil purée to the creamed mixture. Mix well. Melt the chocolate in saucepan or microwave in a glass bowl and add.

Sift flour, baking soda, baking powder, and salt together, add to the chocolate mixture, and blend thoroughly. Pour batter into greased and rice-floured 9″ × 12″ pan. Bake in preheated 350° oven for 30 to 35 minutes, or until center springs back when lightly touched. When cool, frost with your favorite frosting.

This is another cake that tastes good with cream cheese frosting, but for true chocolate lovers, try the Easy Chocolate Icing on page 85.

MOCK BLACK FOREST CAKE

The flavor of this cake with its blend of chocolate, cherries, and liqueur is a winner with my friends. They don't even suspect it's gluten free.

2 cups canned dark cherries	1 cup rice flour
	1/2 cup potato starch flour
2 tablespoons kirschwasser	1 tablespoon soy flour
6 tablespoons (3/4 stick) butter or margarine	3/4 cup sugar
	2 teaspoons baking powder
3/4 cup sour cream or non-dairy substitute	1/2 teaspoon baking soda
	1/2 teaspoon salt
2 eggs, beaten	2 squares baking chocolate

Drain cherries and slice into a small bowl. Cover with liqueur and let stand at least 10 minutes. Melt the butter and add it with the sour cream and eggs to the cherries. Blend well.

In large bowl, combine flours, sugar, baking powder, baking soda, and salt. Add the cherry mixture and stir until moistened. Melt the chocolate and stir into cake batter.

Pour batter into greased and rice-floured 9″ × 5″ × 4″ loaf pan. Bake in preheated 350° oven for 65 to 70 minutes. Cool cake in pan on wire rack for 15 minutes, then remove from pan and cool thoroughly.

Serve with whipped cream. Flavor increases if cake sits overnight.

FRUIT COCKTAIL TORTE

A moist pudding cake that is quick, easy, and delicious. This may be served either hot or cold with whipped cream or whipped nondairy topping. The gluten-free all-purpose flour works well in this heavy cake recipe. My guests never guess the substitution.

1 cup GF flour mix	One 17-ounce can fruit
1 cup sugar	cocktail
1 teaspoon salt	1 teaspoon vanilla
1 teaspoon baking soda	1/2 cup brown sugar
2 eggs, beaten	1/2 cup chopped nuts

In mixing bowl, sift together the flour, sugar, salt, and baking soda.

Add the beaten eggs, fruit cocktail (juice included), and vanilla. Stir until well blended. Pour batter into a greased 9″ × 9″ square pan and sprinkle with the brown sugar and nuts.

Bake 1 hour in preheated 325° oven. Serve warm or cold topped with whipped cream.

For variety, try coconut in place of the chopped nuts.

CARROT CAKE SUPREME

The use of fruit or carrots in a cake almost always ensures success for the gluten-free flours, especially if you use soy flour along with the rice flours. But this cake is even tastier than other recipes I tried. The secret ingredient is the mayonnaise. (You may omit the xanthan gum if you like, but the cake will be more crumbly without it.)

1 1/2 cups rice flour
1/2 cup soy flour
1/2 cup potato starch flour
Optional: 1 teaspoon
    xanthan gum
2 teaspoons baking soda
2 teaspoons cinnamon
1/2 teaspoon powdered
    ginger

1/2 teaspoon salt
4 large eggs
2 cups sugar
1 cup mayonnaise
One 16-ounce can crushed
    pineapple
3 cups grated carrots
1 cup chopped walnuts

In a bowl, stir together the flours, xanthan gum, baking soda, cinnamon, ginger, and salt. Set aside.

In large bowl of the mixer, beat together at medium speed the eggs, sugar, mayonnaise, and pineapple, not drained. Gradually beat in flour mixture until well mixed. With a spoon, stir in carrots and walnuts.

Pour batter into a greased and rice-floured 9″ × 13″ pan. Bake in preheated 350° oven for 45 to 50 minutes, or until cake tester inserted in center comes out clean. Cool in pan.

Serve with whipped cream or frost with cream cheese frosting.

APPLE RAISIN CAKE

A moist, fruity cake that keeps well. The chopped apples and the soy flour add to its moistness. Like the carrot cake, this uses mayonnaise instead of oil or shortening. (Without the xanthan gum the cake will be less springy and will not rise as well.)

2 cups rice flour
1/2 cup soy flour
2 tablespoons potato
  starch flour
Optional: 2 teaspoons
  xanthan gum
2 cups sugar
1 cup mayonnaise
1/3 cup milk or nondairy
  substitute
3 eggs

2 rounded teaspoons
  baking soda
1 1/2 teaspoons cinnamon
1/2 teaspoon nutmeg
1/4 teaspoon ground cloves
1/2 teaspoon salt
3 cups chopped peeled
  apples
1 cup raisins
1/2 cup chopped walnuts

Place in large mixing bowl the flours, xanthan gum, sugar, mayonnaise, milk, eggs, baking soda, spices, and salt. Beat with mixer at low speed for 2 minutes, or 300 strokes by hand. Batter will be very thick.

Stir in apples, raisins and nuts. Spoon batter into greased and rice-floured 9″ × 13″ pan. Bake in preheated 350° oven for 45 minutes, or until tester inserted in center comes out clean. Cool in pan.

Serve with whipped cream or frost with cream cheese frosting.

RAISIN RUM CAKE

This is a real party cake with a rich rum flavor that will please a crowd. Remember to put the raisins to soak in the rum overnight.

1 cup light raisins	1 tablespoon grated lemon
1/3 cup dark rum	peel
2 cups rice flour	1 tablespoon grated orange
1/2 cup tapioca flour	peel
4 teaspoons baking powder	
1 1/2 teaspoons baking soda	*Rum Sauce*
1/2 teaspoon salt	1/2 cup sugar
1/4 teaspoon nutmeg	1/4 cup water
2 teaspoons xanthan gum	2 tablespoons orange juice
1 cup mayonnaise	2 tablespoons lemon juice
1 cup sugar	2 tablespoons dark rum
3 eggs	Optional: 2 tablespoons
1 cup buttermilk	powdered sugar

Soak the raisins in the rum overnight in a covered bowl until they are plump with rum and there is no moisture left in the bowl.

Sift together the flours, baking powder, baking soda, salt, nutmeg, and xanthan gum. Set aside. In mixer bowl, place mayonnaise, sugar, and eggs. Beat together on medium for a few seconds until the eggs are well beaten.

On low speed, add the dry ingredients in 3 additions, alternating with the buttermilk. Then, by hand, stir in the grated lemon and orange peels and rum-soaked raisins.

Pour batter into a greased and rice-floured bundt pan with 10- to 12-cup capacity. Bake in preheated 350° oven for approximately 50 minutes, or until the cake tests done. Let the cake stand in the pan for 10 minutes before turning it out onto a cake plate to add the rum sauce.

RUM SAUCE

In small saucepan, boil together sugar and water for 2 minutes. Remove from heat and stir in the orange juice, lemon juice, and rum.

Using a pastry brush, brush the warm rum sauce over the warm cake. Let cool. Sprinkle the top with powdered sugar, if desired.

COUNTRY JAM CAKE

After a lot of failures with spice cakes, I found this recipe, which comes from the South. It turned out so well that I suspect it was originally made with the rice flours and later converted. As I converted it back, I wondered if this cake originated during the Civil War, when the southern ports were blockaded and no wheat arrived for baking.

The recipe as given below is for a large cake and can easily be halved, in which case use 3 small eggs. It makes great cupcakes that stay moist and do not need frosting.

2 cups rice flour
1/2 cup potato starch flour
1/2 cup tapioca flour
1 teaspoon baking soda
4 teaspoons baking powder
1 teaspoon salt
1 1/2 teaspoons cinnamon
3/4 teaspoon ground cloves
1 teaspoon nutmeg
1 tablespoon xanthan gum

1 cup mayonnaise
1 1/2 cups sugar
5 large eggs
1 cup buttermilk
1 cup raspberry,
   blackberry, or apricot-
   pineapple preserves
1/2 cup chopped pecans or
   walnuts

In a large bowl, combine sifted flours with baking soda, baking powder, salt, spices, and xanthan gum. Set aside.

In mixing bowl, cream mayonnaise and sugar thoroughly with an electric mixer. Add the eggs and beat until the mixture is smooth and silky. Blend in the flour mixture in batches alternating with the buttermilk, after each addition beating by hand with a large spoon or rubber spatula. Stir in the jam and nuts.

Spoon the mixture into 2 greased and rice-floured 9″ round cake pans or a large 9″ × 13″ oblong pan. Bake in preheated 350° oven for 35 minutes for the round pans or 45 minutes for the oblong pan. Since the difference in the thickness of the jam used will make a difference in the timing, test the cake for doneness. The testing tooth-pick should come out clean.

This cake can be served with whipped cream, cream cheese frost-ing, or any purchased frosting you choose.

ANGEL FOOD CAKE

An angel-light cake with a delicate mix of flours. I almost gave up on this one until I hit upon this successful formula.

7 egg whites ($^3/_4$ cup)	$^3/_4$ teaspoon cream of
$^1/_2$ cup powdered sugar	tartar
$^1/_4$ cup potato starch flour	$^1/_4$ teaspoon salt
$^1/_4$ cup cornstarch	1 teaspoon dried lemon
$^1/_3$ cup granulated sugar	peel

Set the egg whites aside to bring to room temperature.

Sift together into a small bowl the powdered sugar, flour, and cornstarch. The sifting is essential in this recipe. Measure your gran-ulated sugar to have handy.

In large glass or metal (not plastic) mixing bowl, place egg whites, cream of tartar, salt, and lemon peel. With mixer at high, beat until the mixture is well blended. Continue to beat, adding the granulated sugar slowly. Beat just until sugar is dissolved and whites form stiff peaks.

With a rubber spatula, gently fold in the flour and powdered sugar mixture about one-fourth at a time, folding just enough so the flour disappears.

Pour batter into ungreased 9″ tube pan and cut through with spatula to break any air bubbles. Bake 35 minutes in preheated 375° oven, or until top springs back when lightly touched. Remove from oven and cool the cake in the inverted pan. Remove cake only when completely cool.

This recipe can be doubled for large 10″ tube pan.

CHEESECAKES

These are so easy to make that no cook should be afraid to try. I give three different cheesecake recipes; all can use the following crust.

CRUST

   2 cups GF cereal or GF dried bread or cookie crumbs
   3 tablespoons melted butter or margarine
   2 tablespoons sugar
   1/4 teaspoon cinnamon
   1/4 teaspoon nutmeg

Crush the cereal or crumbs, add remaining ingredients, and mix together in a bowl or shake together in a plastic bag. Pat out into a 10″ springform pan or large pie plate, reserving a tablespoon to top the cheesecake before baking, if desired.

SIMPLY SCRUMPTIOUS CHEESECAKE

A rich, never-fail cheesecake that can be eaten alone or with a topping of simple crushed fruit, either fresh or canned.

   Three 8-ounce packages   1 cup sugar
      cream cheese   1 teaspoon vanilla
   4 eggs

Soften cream cheese and combine with eggs, sugar, and vanilla. Beat with electric mixer until well blended. Pour into prepared crust and top with remaining crumb mixture. Bake in preheated 375° oven for 35 to 40 minutes, or until set.

When cool, refrigerate several hours before serving with or without toppings. This is a large cake and very rich, so it will serve 12.

For a lighter version of this cake, use two 8-ounce packages cream cheese and 1 cup cottage cheese.

ORANGE CHEESECAKE

A nice blend of flavors for both orange and cheesecake lovers. This is a smaller recipe than the preceding one so you can cut the crust mixture in half and pat into a small (7") pie plate.

Two 3-ounce packages cream cheese	1 teaspoon grated orange peel
1 egg	3 tablespoons orange juice
1/3 cup sugar	1/4 teaspoon vanilla
1/3 cup sour cream or nondairy substitute	1/4 cup orange marmalade for topping

Soften the cream cheese. Place in mixing bowl and blend with egg, sugar, and sour cream until the mixture is smooth. Add orange peel, orange juice, and vanilla.

Pour the mixture into prepared crust and bake in preheated 375° oven for about 30 to 35 minutes or until set. Remove from oven and cool slightly while heating the marmalade in a saucepan or in microwave for 1/2 to 1 minute. Spoon this over top of cheesecake and refrigerate at least 3 hours. *Makes 6 servings.*

LINDA'S LIGHTER CHEESECAKE

A very light cheesecake with delicate fruit flavors. This is a large recipe so prepare two 8" square pans or one 9" × 13" oblong pan with crust mixture suggested previously reserving some, again, for topping. Since this is a no-bake cheesecake you can put the crust in a preheated oven at 375° for about 5 to 7 minutes to brown slightly, though it is not necessary.

One 6-ounce package
  lemon gelatin (see Note)
1 cup hot water
One 9-ounce can crushed
  pineapple (see Note)
16 ounces large-curd
  cottage cheese

1 cup dry milk powder
$^{1}/_{2}$ cup ice water
3 tablespoons lemon juice
$^{1}/_{2}$ cup sugar
1$^{1}/_{2}$ to 2 tablespoons
  grated lemon rind

Keep ingredients cold at all times.

Dissolve the gelatin in hot water and chill until slightly thickened.

Meanwhile, drain pineapple and save the juice. Beat cottage cheese with electric mixer at low speed until very creamy. When gelatin has thickened, beat the cottage cheese into the gelatin and place in refrigerator.

Mix milk powder, ice water, and lemon juice. Beat until fluffy and stiff. Combine with slightly thickened gelatin and cheese mixture and beat at high speed. Add pineapple juice and sugar slowly, beating thoroughly. Fold in pineapple and lemon rind. Pour over crumb crust and top with remaining crumbs. Chill in refrigerator 2 to 4 hours.

NOTE: Orange or peach gelatin may be used, and other fresh fruit may be substituted for the pineapple, but do not substitute fresh pineapple for canned, or the gelatin will not set.

INDIVIDUAL CAKES

CREAM PUFFS

Don't be put off by the elegance of this dessert. It is one of the easiest to make with our flours. Try it; impress your guests.

1 cup water	1/2 teaspoon salt
1/2 cup shortening	1 tablespoon sugar
1/3 cup potato starch flour	4 eggs
2/3 cup rice flour	

Combine water and shortening in large saucepan. Bring to rapid boil. Mix flours, salt, and sugar and add to water and shortening. Stir until mixture forms a ball that leaves the sides of the pan. Remove from heat and cool slightly.

Add the unbeaten eggs, one at a time, beating well with electric mixer after each egg is added.

Drop by tablespoonfuls onto greased cookie tin. The puffs should be approximately 2 inches round and about 1 1/2 inches high. Leave space for them to expand. Bake 20 minutes in preheated 450° oven, then reduce heat to 350° and bake for 20 minutes more. Remove from oven and prick with knife to let steam escape.

Serve cold filled with sweetened whipped cream. *Makes 8 to 10 puffs.*

CHOCOLATE ECLAIRS

Another chou pastry dessert sure to please all guests. These can be made ahead and filled just before serving. Bake cream puff dough in elongated (finger) shapes by molding with damp rubber spatula or pressing out of a pastry bag.

1 recipe Cream Puffs, page 82

Filling

1 cup cream or nondairy substitute
3 egg yolks
1/4 cup sugar
3 tablespoons sweet rice flour

1 tablespoon butter or margarine
1 tablespoon rum

Glaze

2 ounces semisweet chocolate
1 tablespoon coffee
1 1/2 tablespoons butter or margarine

Heat the cream but do not boil. Set aside.

In saucepan, whip egg yolks and gradually beat in the sugar. Continue beating until the mixture is thick and lemon-colored. Slowly add flour, then heated cream.

Put saucepan over moderate heat and cook, stirring slowly, until the custard comes to a boil. If it starts to lump, beat vigorously. Cook about 3 minutes.

Remove from heat. Stir in butter and rum. Chill covered with plastic wrap to keep a skin from forming on the surface. Stir before filling the eclairs. (Do this 4 hours or less before serving so the eclairs will not become soggy.)

For the glaze, melt the chocolate and beat in the coffee and butter. Spread lightly on the eclairs. *Makes 8 to 10 eclairs.*

PECAN BROWNIE CUPCAKES

These rich, fudgy brownies are baked as cupcakes, which keeps them moist. The single serving size is great for freezing for lunches or serving in single portions to the dieter. For the true chocoholic, ice with the chocolate frosting on page 85.

3 ounces baking chocolate	1 teaspoon vanilla
³/₄ cup (1 ¹/₂ sticks) butter or margarine	³/₄ cup GF flour mix
1 cup brown sugar	1 cup chopped pecans
¹/₂ cup granulated sugar	Optional: 16 to 18 pecan halves for garnish
3 large eggs	

In a 2- or 3-quart saucepan, combine chocolate and butter. Place over low heat and stir occasionally until melted. Remove from heat. Stir in brown and granulated sugars. Beat in eggs, one at a time. Add vanilla. Beat in flour. Stir in chopped nuts.

Spoon batter into paper-lined 2¹/₂″ muffin cups, filling about two-thirds full. If desired, place a pecan half on top of each. Bake in preheated 350° oven for 22 to 25 minutes. Tops should look crackly but interiors should still be slightly moist. Let cool in pan for 15 minutes, then remove and let cool on rack. *Makes 16 to 18 cupcakes.*

FROSTINGS

CREAM CHEESE FROSTING

There are several prepared cream cheese frostings on the market that are gluten free. But this is simple to make if you haven't a packaged one on hand.

One 8-ounce package cream cheese, softened
1/2 cup (1 stick) butter or margarine, softened
1 teaspoon vanilla
One 1-pound box confectioner's sugar

Combine cream cheese, butter, and vanilla in a mixing bowl. Blend at low speed with electric mixer. Gradually add powdered sugar, beating until fluffy. You may add a few drops of cream, if necessary, to make spreading easier.

This makes a large recipe, enough for the tops of two 9″ × 13″ oblong cakes, but the frosting keeps in the refrigerator for days. Or better yet, freeze the balance for the next cake.

EASY CHOCOLATE ICING

Again, you may buy gluten-free chocolate frosting on the market but this is an easy one. It keeps well in the refrigerator for several days and freezes well. Warm to room temperature to spread on cake or cupcakes.

4 squares baking chocolate
1/2 cup (1 stick) butter or margarine
One 1-pound box confectioner's sugar
1 teaspoon vanilla
1/2 cup milk (approximately)

Melt chocolate in a saucepan over very low heat, stirring constantly. (Or melt in microwave in a glass bowl.)

Stir butter to soften. Beat in half the sugar. Blend in the chocolate and vanilla. Add the remaining sugar alternately with the milk, beating until smooth and of the right consistency to spread. *Makes 2 1/2 cups icing.*

PENUCHE FROSTING

This butterscotch-tasting frosting is especially good on spice or chocolate cakes. It's a bit more trouble than the preceding two but well worth it.

2 cups brown sugar
1/2 cup milk or nondairy liquid
1/2 cup (1 stick) margarine

Place ingredients in a saucepan and stir over low heat until margarine is melted. Then bring rapidly to a full boil, stirring constantly. Boil to 220° on a candy thermometer, or exactly 1 minute. Remove from heat.

Beat until lukewarm and of the right consistency to spread. If frosting gets too hard, it can be thinned with a little cream. *Makes approximately 1 1/2 cups icing or enough for 1 cake.*

PIES AND PASTRY

The fruit or cream fillings for many pies are gluten free. There are many recipes we can find in our old cookbooks; but the catch is the pastry. Every recipe calls for pastry flour, which means wheat.

Working with rice flour is more difficult than wheat flour, but not impossible. And it makes a delicious pastry. I've also suggested other easier ones such as cereal or crumb crusts. In addition, I've included a few of my favorite pie recipes, but in most cases you can use your own recipes for fruit pies as long as you remember to thicken with tapioca, rice flour, or cornstarch. If you see a cream pie recipe you think sounds good, check to see if it is thickened with egg yolks or cornstarch rather than wheat flour.

There are also many packaged pudding and pie fillings that are gluten free. Be sure to read the ingredient list on the box each time, for manufacturers do change formulas and one that is safe for you one day may include wheat starch the next time you buy it.

PASTRY AND CRUSTS

TENDER VINEGAR PASTRY

This is a tender, tasty pastry for either a 2-crust pie or for 2 single crusts. This pastry crumbles when cut and served warm but works well for cold serving. If you wish to serve the pie warm, cool it, cut, and then reheat the pie wedges on their serving dish in the microwave or oven.

1 1/2 cups rice flour	1 teaspoon xanthan gum*
1/2 cup potato starch flour	3/4 cup shortening
1/4 cup tapioca flour	1 egg, lightly beaten
1 teaspoon salt	2 tablespoons vinegar
1 tablespoon sugar	2 tablespoons cold water

Sift the flours, salt, sugar, and xanthan gum into a mixing bowl. Cut in the shortening. Blend together the beaten egg, vinegar, and cold water. Stir them into the flour mix. This will seem quite moist, but a rice crust needs to be more moist than a wheat flour one.

Knead the mixture into a ball (handling will not toughen the dough). Separate into 2 balls and roll, one at a time, between 2 sheets of plastic wrap. To place in pie tin, remove top sheet and, using the other for ease of handling, invert the dough and drop it into the pan, shaping into the curves before removing the second piece of plastic wrap. To bake crust to be used later, bake in preheated 450° oven for 10 to 12 minutes. For a filled pie, follow directions for that pie.

*The xanthan gum may be omitted but it helps give the pastry stretch.

CRUMB CRUST

A good use for the crumbs from your baking mistakes. Dry GF bread, cake, or cookie pieces in 200° oven until crisp and dry, 1 or 2 hours. Then pulverize in a food processor. Store in your freezer to pull out when needed. The following recipe makes enough dough for a 10" springform pan or to line an 8" pie pan. Increase all measurements slightly for a deep 9" pie tin.

1 1/2 cups GF crumbs
1 tablespoon sugar
1 teaspoon cinnamon

1/4 cup melted butter or margarine

Put all the ingredients in a 1-gallon plastic food storage bag. Shake together to mix. Press the dough evenly onto the bottom and sides of the greased pie pan or the bottom of the springform pan.

If the pie is to be baked, fill before baking. If the pie filling is already cooked (cream pie, lemon, package mix, and so on), then bake your crust in preheated 400° oven for about 8 minutes before filling.

CEREAL CRUST

Probably the easiest of all crusts. I make this crust in the same plastic bag in which I crush the cereal, thus eliminating one bowl to wash.

2 cups GF cereal
3 tablespoons melted butter or margarine
2 tablespoons sugar

Crush the cereal in a plastic bag, then add the butter and sugar and shake together. Pat the mixture into a 9" pie tin. If the pie is to be baked, pour the mixture into the unbaked cereal crust and bake according to the filling recipe. If the pie filling is already cooked, bake the crust in preheated 400° oven for about 6 minutes before filling it. Cool before serving.

GINGER COOKIE CRUST

On page 62, you'll find a recipe for Ginger-Almond Sticks. If you have any crumbs or broken pieces from this recipe, save them for this crust for a truly gourmet pie or cheesecake. It's worth making the cookies just for the crumbs. Make and bake a whole recipe and store the crumbs for crusts.

For a 9″ pie you'll need 1 1/2 cups of crumbs and 2 1/2 tablespoons of melted margarine or butter, a little less of each for an 8″ pie. If you are short of crumbs, you can use 1/2 cup crushed cornflakes to make up the difference.

MERINGUE SHELL

A sweet, frothy shell for light, fluffy pies.

2 egg whites	1/4 teaspoon salt
1/4 teaspoon cream of	1/2 teaspoon vanilla
tartar	1/2 cup sugar

Place the egg whites, cream of tartar, salt, and vanilla in a mixing bowl and beat with electric mixer until foamy. Then, beating constantly, add the sugar about a tablespoon at a time. Continue beating until very stiff and glossy. Grease a deep 9″ pie pan and spread the mixture on the sides and bottom. Bake in preheated 275° oven for 1 hour. Cool away from drafts before filling.

REFRIGERATOR PIES AND
MERINGUE-TOPPED PIES

ANGEL PIE (PINEAPPLE)

A melt-in-your-mouth dessert.

Meringue Shell, page 92
3/4 cup sugar
1/4 cup cornstarch
1/2 teaspoon salt
One 20-ounce can crushed
   pineapple

2 tablespoons lemon juice
2 tablespoons butter or
   margarine
2 egg yolks, slightly beaten
1 cup whipping cream or
   nondairy liquid

Prepare and bake the meringue shell.

Combine sugar, cornstarch, and salt in a saucepan. Gradually stir in the pineapple and its juice, lemon juice, and butter. Cook over medium heat, stirring constantly, until thickened. Gradually add a little of the hot pineapple to the egg yolks, then combine this mixture with the hot mixture in the saucepan.

Cook 1 or 2 minutes more, stirring constantly. Chill until cold. Whip the cream and fold into the pineapple mixture. Pour into the meringue shell. Refrigerate until serving time.

For variation, substitute one 12-ounce carton Cranberry Orange Sauce plus 1/3 cup orange juice for the pineapple. Or, substitute one 17-ounce can apricot halves, drained and puréed, plus 1/3 cup reserved drained juice.

BASIC CREAM PIE FILLING

This rich filling will satisfy anyone's craving for cream pie. Use it with bananas, pineapple, or with GF canned-fruit pie fillings. Prepare the desired single crust for a 9" pie (cereal, crumb, or vinegar pastry) and bake according to the recipe. Then make the filling.

2 cups cream or nondairy substitute	1 cup sugar
	1/2 cup rice flour
6 egg yolks	1/2 teaspoon salt

Place all ingredients in the top of a double boiler. Mix and continue stirring over gently simmering water until thick. Remove from stove and flavor with one of the following fruits.

BANANA CREAM PIE: Line the baked pie shell with 2 bananas cut into 1/4-inch slices. Pour the cream filling over the bananas. Chill and decorate with whipped cream fluted around the edges before serving.

PINEAPPLE CREAM PIE: Add an 8-ounce can crushed pineapple, drained, to the cream filling before pouring into the baked pie shell. Chill and decorate as above with whipped cream at edges.

COCONUT CREAM PIE: Add 1 cup sweetened flake coconut to the pie filling while it is still hot. Pour into the baked shell. Top with a meringue of 2 egg whites beaten stiff with 2 tablespoons sugar. Drizzle on a couple of tablespoons of coconut. Bake in preheated 425° oven until meringue browns. Watch carefully; don't let meringue get too dark.

LEMON LEMON PIE

I gave this pie its name because it has a tart lemon flavor. It is not too wicked in calories, since there is no thickening added. For this pie I like to use a baked vinegar pastry crust, but you may opt for the ginger cookie crust instead. It is terrific with this filling.

10 eggs   1 cup lemon juice
2 1/2 cups sugar   Grated rind of 2 lemons
1/4 teaspoon salt

Separate 6 of the eggs, putting the yolks in the top of a double boiler and the whites in a bowl for beating later. Add the remaining 4 whole eggs to the double boiler. Add 2 cups of the sugar, salt, and lemon juice. Place over hot water on the stove and stir with a wooden spoon until the custard is thick. Remove from heat and add the lemon rind.

Beat the 6 egg whites until stiff, and very gradually add the remaining 1/2 cup sugar. Fold one-third of the egg whites into the cooled custard. Pour this into a baked pie crust. Cover with the remaining egg white meringue and put under the broiler until lightly browned.

BOSTON CREAM PIE

Now this cake-pie combination is not forbidden fruit for the gluten intolerant.

1 recipe Classic Sponge Cake, page 69
1/2 recipe Basic Cream Pie Filling, page 94
One 27-ounce can GF prepared fruit pie filling (cherry,
    berry, apple, or other)
Whipped cream topping or a nondairy substitute

Prepare the sponge cake recipe and bake it in two 8″ round cake pans. They will take about 10 to 15 minutes less time to bake than in a tube pan. Remove from pans to cool on wire racks.

Spread one layer with the cream pie filling. Top with the second cake layer and top this with the prepared fruit pie filling. Make a decorative edge around the outside of top with whipped cream or nondairy topping. Refrigerate.

Cut into wedges to serve. This is a rich pie and can easily be cut to serve 12.

NOTE: Instead of canned pie filling, you may use fresh fruit, cooked and sweetened to taste and thickened with 1 to 2 tablespoons sweet rice flour. You will need 1 1/2 to 2 cups fruit filling.

BAKED PIES

RAISIN-SOUR CREAM PIE

An old favorite that's quick to make; it will disappear just as fast. You may use a regular pastry crust or cereal or crumb crust for this pie. If you use a cereal crust, you might like to add 1 teaspoon of cinnamon to the cereal before crushing. Prepare the crust but don't bake it. Prepare the following filling:

3 eggs	1/4 teaspoon cloves
1 1/4 cups sugar	1 1/2 cups sour cream or
1/4 teaspoon salt	nondairy substitute
1 teaspoon cinnamon	1 1/2 cups seedless raisins

Beat together eggs, sugar, salt, cinnamon, and cloves. Then blend in the sour cream or nondairy substitute. Stir in the raisins.

Pour into a pastry-lined 9″ pie tin. Bake in preheated 450° oven for 10 minutes, then turn to 325° for 20 to 25 minutes, or until a knife inserted in the center comes out clean. Serve slightly warm or cold. Refrigerate if kept more than several hours after baking.

APPLE PEAR DELUXE PIE

You can use any of your favorite recipes for regular apple pie, but this will be a change for the palate.

Tender Vinegar Pastry,
    page 90
4 cups peeled, diced tart
    apples
1 cup plus $1/2$ teaspoon
    sugar
2 tablespoons tapioca flour

$1/8$ teaspoon salt
$1/2$ teaspoon cinnamon
4 canned pear halves
2 tablespoons rum
2 tablespoons butter or
    margarine
1 tablespoon milk

Prepare pastry and fit half into a 9″ pie pan.

Place apples in a large mixing bowl. Mix 1 cup sugar, tapioca flour, salt, and cinnamon, and add to the apples, tumbling to coat thoroughly. Set aside.

Crush the pears and spread the pulp in the bottom of your pastry-lined pan. Sprinkle with rum. Pour the apple mixture over the pears and dot with butter. Add the top crust, seal, and crimp edges. Cut slits for vents. Brush the top of the pastry with milk and sprinkle on about $1/2$ teaspoon of sugar. Bake in preheated 400° oven for 45 minutes, or until the apples are tender. Serve warm. *Makes 8 servings.*

Because this pastry cuts better cold, you might want to let the pie cool, then cut the wedges and place on dessert plates to reheat in the microwave before serving.

PECAN PIE

A southern favorite—easy to make, high in calories. Serve small portions, for this is a rich pie. The texture of a cereal crust goes well with this. If you use it, try chopping a couple of tablespoons of the nuts very fine and adding them to the crust mixture before patting into the pie tin.

3 eggs
1 cup dark corn syrup
1 cup brown sugar
1 teaspoon vanilla

2 tablespoons margarine,
  melted
1 1/2 cups pecan bits or
  halves

In mixing bowl, beat the eggs. Add the corn syrup, sugar, vanilla, and melted margarine. Stir together until blended. Fold in the pecans. Pour into an unbaked pie shell and bake in preheated 350° oven for 50 to 55 minutes, until knife inserted near center comes out clean. Cool before serving. *Makes a large 9" pie that can serve 8 to 10.*

RUM PECAN PIE

Rum gives a new taste to the preceding pie. Prepare an unbaked crust, either the cereal or crumb crust, omitting the sugar.

2 eggs
2/3 cup brown sugar
2/3 cup dark corn syrup
1/3 cup dark rum

2 tablespoons butter or
  margarine, melted
1 teaspoon vanilla
2 cups broken pecans

Break eggs into a mixing bowl. Beat slightly. Add the rest of the ingredients except the nuts. Beat until well blended. Then fold in the nuts. Pour into the unbaked pie shell and bake in preheated 425° oven for 45 to 50 minutes.

TROPICAL TOFU PIE

The blend of several tropical fruit flavors plus the tofu makes this a welcome dessert that is not too sweet. It tastes a bit like a light cheesecake. This is served cold, so it can be made ahead. Prepare a deep 9" cereal or crumb crust, using ¹/₂ teaspoon cinnamon for added flavor if desired. Do not bake the crust.

One 14-ounce block firm
  or medium tofu
3 eggs
²/₃ cup sugar
2 teaspoons grated orange
  peel

2 tablespoons lemon
  juice
2 ripe bananas
One 8-ounce can crushed
  pineapple

Place the tofu, broken into chunks, in a food processor. Process lightly. Add eggs, sugar, orange peel, and lemon juice. Process until well mixed. Then add the bananas, cut into chunks, and process until smooth. Stir in the well-drained crushed pineapple. Pour into the prepared crust.

Bake in preheated 350° oven for about 45 to 50 minutes, or until center is firm. Cool. Refrigerate until served. The pie may be served plain or with whipped cream or crushed fruit as topping. *Makes 8 to 10 servings.*

LEMON SPONGE PIE

A very different lemon pie with a delightful tart taste, this is simple to make but turns out layered with a frothy, creamy top.

Tender Vinegar Pastry, page 90	2 tablespoons sweet rice flour
3 eggs	1/4 teaspoon salt
3 tablespoons butter or margarine	1 1/2 cups buttermilk
3/4 cup sugar	3 tablespoons lemon juice

Prepare pastry and use half to line 9″ pie shell, reserving remaining pastry for another use.

Separate the eggs, putting the yolks in large mixing bowl and the whites in small one. Melt the butter and set aside. Beat the yolks with electric mixer and add 1/2 cup of the sugar, rice flour, and salt. Stir in the melted butter, buttermilk, and lemon juice.

Beat the egg whites until they form peaks, and gradually beat in the remaining 1/4 cup sugar. Fold these into the yolk mix. Pour into the prepared pie shell. Bake in preheated 350° oven for 20 to 25 minutes, or until knife inserted in center comes out clean.

BREAKFAST AND BRUNCH

There is no reason a gluten-free diet should be restricted at breakfast or brunch. Pancakes, waffles, and coffee cakes can all be made without wheat. And they can be so good the rest of the family will enjoy them, too.

In the following section you'll find a wide variety of breakfast and brunch favorites, ranging from a gluten-free muesli to Toad-in-the-Hole.

Again I use the gluten-free flour mix, which I make up ahead of time in large quantities, in many of the recipes, since I find the combination of flours gives a good texture and flavor. The formula for the GF flour mix is:

2 parts white rice flour
$2/3$ part potato starch flour
$1/3$ part tapioca flour

MUESLI

There are several gluten-free cereals on the market but none combine fruit, grain, and protein as does this mixture, which will give variety to the breakfast menu.

3 cups gluten-free puffed rice
1 cup Perky's Nutty Rice cereal
3 cups gluten-free cornflakes
1 cup roasted soy nuts, peanuts, coconut, or almonds

1 cup sunflower seeds
1 cup each of any 2:
  currants or raisins
  dried date bits
  dried banana flakes
  dried cherries or apples
  dried peach or apricot bits

Simply toss all ingredients together and store in plastic freezer bags. (No need to freeze, but the freezer bags are thicker.) Great for a hasty breakfast at home or to take on trips so you can have a gluten-free breakfast cereal when there is none on the menu. *Makes 10 cups muesli.*

ENGLISH MUFFINS

These yeasty breakfast crumpets are easy to make, since you bake them with only 1 rising. They turn out heavy, flat circles of bread that look, smell, and taste like those containing wheat. These freeze well and are an excellent bread for traveling. They also make a fine base for the Shrimp Cheese Spread found on page 120.

You will need 12 English muffin rings. Or you can substitute 4-inch flat tuna fish cans by removing both ends. If you wish to try the recipe before investing in baking tins, roll out the dough and cut in circles with a 4-inch glass or can and bake the circles on a greased baking sheet.

2 cups rice flour
2 cups tapioca
   flour
2/3 cup dried milk or
   powdered baby formula,
   page x
3 1/2 teaspoons xanthan
   gum
1 teaspoon salt

2 yeast cakes, or 2
   tablespoons dry yeast
   granules
1 cup lukewarm water
1 tablespoon sugar
3 tablespoons shortening
1/2 cup hot water
4 egg whites, at room
   temperature

Put flours, dried milk, xanthan gum, and salt in mixer bowl. Crumble the yeast into the lukewarm water with the sugar added. Melt the shortening in the hot water.

In mixing bowl, blend the dry ingredients on low. Pour in the hot water and shortening, blending to mix. Add the egg whites, blend again, then add the yeast mixture. Beat on high speed for 4 minutes.

Spoon half the dough onto a rice-floured board or rice-floured wax paper. Sprinkle some rice flour over the top and then roll out to 1/2-inch thickness. Cut circles with the English muffin tins or your substitute. With a spatula, lift the dough and tins together and place on greased baking sheets. Repeat with the second half of the dough. Let rise, covered, for 40 to 60 minutes.

Put the sheets into a preheated 350° oven. Bake for 20 minutes, then, with a spatula, turn the muffins (tins and all) over. Bake another 20 minutes (40 minutes altogether).

Remove from cookie sheets to rack to cool. (You may remove the rings while they are hot.) *Makes twelve 4-inch muffins.*

BUTTERMILK PANCAKES

When a gourmet friend said she never made pancakes unless she had buttermilk on hand, I thought of trying to create a recipe with our gluten-free flour. She declared these a success. (I didn't tell her that I used powdered buttermilk.) You can use all rice flour instead of the GF flour mix, if you prefer.

1 cup GF flour mix	1/2 teaspoon salt
1/4 cup buttermilk powder	2 eggs
1 tablespoon sugar	1 cup water
1 teaspoon baking powder	2 tablespoons vegetable oil
1/2 teaspoon baking soda	

Sift the dry ingredients together into a mixing bowl. Beat the eggs with the water and oil, and add. Beat until batter is smooth, but do not overbeat.

Drop from mixing spoon onto a hot greased griddle and cook until top is full of tiny bubbles and the underside is brown. Turn and brown on the other side. *Makes ten 4-inch pancakes.* (Recipe can easily be doubled.)

RICE-RICOTTA PANCAKES

A crêpelike pancake with delicate texture and flavor—delicious. This batter can be made either in a food processor or with an electric mixer. For a thicker pancake, reduce the milk to 1/2 cup.

2 eggs	1 teaspoon baking powder
1/2 cup ricotta cheese	1/2 teaspoon salt
1 tablespoon vegetable oil	3/4 cup milk or nondairy
1/2 cup rice flour	liquid
2 teaspoons sugar	

Beat together the eggs and ricotta cheese and add the oil. In a large measuring cup, mix flour, sugar, baking powder, and salt. Beat into egg mixture alternately with the milk. The mixture will be thin. Pour onto either lightly greased or Teflon griddle and bake at medium high. (Too hot a griddle will burn the pancakes.) *Makes 1 dozen 4-inch pancakes.*

BUTTERMILK WAFFLES

An easy-to-make waffle for the whole family. No one will guess it is gluten free. The baked waffles freeze well, to be used later under creamed meat sauces or as a shortcake for fruit.

1 1/4 cups GF flour mix*	1 tablespoon sugar
1/4 cup buttermilk powder	3 tablespoons shortening
2 teaspoons baking powder	2 eggs
1 teaspoon baking soda	1 cup water
1/2 teaspoon salt	

Sift the dry ingredients into a mixing bowl. Cut in the shortening until the mixture is very fine. In another bowl, beat the eggs and water. Add these to the dry ingredients. Beat just until the batter is smooth; do not overbeat. Bake on a hot waffle iron. *Makes 3 or 4 waffles.*

*All white rice flour may be used, or a combination of 3/4 cup rice flour and 1/2 cup corn flour. Each makes a slightly different-tasting waffle.

RICE-SOY WAFFLES

A light, crisp waffle, easy to make.

1 cup rice flour	1 tablespoon sugar
1/2 cup soy flour	3 eggs
1/2 cup potato starch flour	1/4 cup vegetable oil
1/2 teaspoon salt	1 1/2 cups milk or nondairy
5 teaspoons baking powder	liquid

Measure dry ingredients, mix together, and set aside.

In mixing bowl, beat eggs, oil, and liquid. Add dry ingredients and fold in gently with spoon. Don't overbeat.

Bake on a heated waffle iron and serve. These freeze if there are any left over. After being frozen, they are slightly heavier and a little less crisp but still good. *Makes 6 to 8 waffles.*

CRÊPES

Don't be put off by the French name for these easy, make-ahead pancakes, which can be packed with various fillings to suit different tastes. They may be breakfast blintzes, fruit desserts, or a substantial brunch or luncheon main dish. Make these and freeze them to pull out anytime you want a special breakfast or brunch treat.

2/3 cup GF flour mix	1 1/2 cups milk or nondairy liquid
1/2 teaspoon salt	2 tablespoons butter,
3 eggs	melted

Place flour, salt, and eggs in a medium bowl. Whisk together or mix with hand eggbeater until smooth. Slowly beat in the milk and melted butter. Place bowl in the refrigerator and let rest 1 to 2 hours.

Using a 7″ skillet or crêpe pan, heat a small amount of oil and pour in 1/4 cup batter, or spoon in approximately 3 tablespoons or enough for a very thin covering. You may have to tilt the pan to coat the entire bottom. Cook until the bottom of the crêpe is golden brown and the edges curl, then turn, barely cooking the reverse side. Slip the crêpe onto wax paper. Repeat the process until all the batter is used. (If you have a Teflon pan, oil only for the first crêpe.) *Makes about 1 dozen 7-inch crêpes.*

The crêpes can now be frozen for later use (remember to place wax paper between them for easy separation). Or you may proceed to fill the crêpes with any desired filling.

BREAKFAST BLINTZES

Cheese blintzes, a Jewish-American favorite, make a wonderfully refreshing change from jam or syrup on pancakes. These can be made ahead and heated up in the oven or microwave for a treat at breakfast.

> 1 batch (about 12) prepared Crêpes (page 108)
> 1 cup cottage or ricotta cheese
> One 3-ounce package cream cheese, softened
> 1/4 cup sugar
> 1 teaspoon lemon juice

Mix together in a bowl the cheeses, sugar, and lemon juice.

Fill the crêpes by spooning about a tablespoon of the mixture into the center of each. Roll up and place seam side down in an 8″ × 12″ glass baking dish. Or you may fold the other sides in, making small packets or squares. Repeat with all 12 crêpes (or as many as you plan to make). Heat in preheated 350° oven for about 15 minutes or in the microwave on medium until heated through. Serve topped with fresh or frozen and thawed fruit or berries. *Makes 1 dozen blintzes.*

CHICKEN CRÊPES

A make-ahead dish for brunch or lunch that can be taken from the refrigerator and popped into the oven half an hour before serving time. The special flavor comes from the light ginger and curry seasonings. These go well with a combination of sliced fruits.

1 batch (about 12) prepared Crêpes (page 108)	2 teaspoons curry powder
	1/2 teaspoon grated fresh ginger
4 tablespoons (1/2 stick) margarine	1 cup chicken broth
2 tablespoons chopped onion	3 cups diced cooked chicken
2 tablespoons rice flour	1/2 cup sour cream or nondairy substitute
1/2 teaspoon salt	2 tablespoons butter, melted
Dash of garlic salt	
1 1/2 teaspoons sugar	

Melt the margarine in a large frying pan. Add the onion and sauté until tender. Stir in the rice flour, salt, garlic salt, sugar, curry, and grated ginger. Cook a minute or two, then add the broth and bring to a simmer until thickened. Add the chicken and sour cream and heat a few seconds before removing from the stove.

Butter a 9″ × 13″ baking dish. Place 1 or 2 heaping tablespoons of the chicken curry in the center of each crêpe. Roll the crêpe and place seam side down in the buttered dish. Repeat until the dish is full, packing them tightly. Drizzle with melted butter. Bake 20 to 25 minutes in preheated 375° oven, or until hot and bubbling. *Makes 6 servings.*

CRANBERRY-PLUS
COFFEE CAKE

This springy, moist coffee cake can change flavors with whatever fruit you add to the cranberries in the recipe. I have made it successfully with chopped apples, chopped moist dried prunes, grated carrots, grated zucchini, and drained crushed pineapple. Good enough to eat as bar cookies or a square topped with whipped cream for dessert.

2 large eggs
3/4 cup sugar
1/3 cup mayonnaise
1/2 cup rice flour
1/4 cup soy flour
1/4 cup potato starch flour
1/2 teaspoon xanthan gum
1 teaspoon pumpkin pie spice

1 teaspoon baking powder
1/4 teaspoon baking soda
1 cup fresh or frozen cranberries
1 cup chopped fruit or grated vegetable
1/2 cup chopped pecans, walnuts, or macadamia nuts

In mixing bowl, beat together eggs, sugar, and mayonnaise.

Mix together the flours, xanthan gum, spice, baking powder, and baking soda. Stir into the egg mixture, blending well. Stir in the whole cranberries, chopped fruit or grated vegetable, and nuts.

Spread batter into a greased 9″ × 9″ pan. Bake in preheated 350° oven until cake feels firm when touched in center and edges begin to pull from pan, about 45 minutes. Cut into squares and serve either warm or cool. Can be made ahead and kept covered with plastic wrap for up to 3 days.

APPLE BUNDT COFFEE CAKE

The surprise is the apple filling in the center of this rich bundt cake. The xanthan gum is optional; the cake texture will be firmer and less crumbly if you use it.

1 to 2 large apples (2 cups sliced)	3 eggs
1/4 cup apple juice	1/2 teaspoon vanilla
1 tablespoon cornstarch	1 cup sour cream or nondairy substitute
1/2 teaspoon cinnamon	1 1/2 cups GF flour mix
1/4 teaspoon nutmeg	1/2 teaspoon xanthan gum
3/4 cup plus 1 tablespoon sugar	2 teaspoons baking powder
1/3 cup shortening	1/2 teaspoon baking soda
	1/2 teaspoon salt

Peel, core, and slice the apples. Place in a microwave dish and toss apple slices with the juice, cornstarch, cinnamon, and nutmeg plus the 1 tablespoon sugar. Cover with plastic wrap and microwave on high 6 to 7 minutes, stirring once or twice. (If you do not have a microwave, use 3/4 cup thick applesauce, adding the cinnamon and nutmeg.) Set aside while you make the batter.

Cream 3/4 cup sugar and shortening until light. Beat in the eggs and vanilla, then add the sour cream. Next, stir in the flour mixed with the xanthan gum, baking powder, baking soda, and salt.

Pour half the batter into the bottom of a well-greased bundt pan. Over it arrange the apple mixture, keeping it from the edges of the pan. Top with the rest of the batter. Bake in preheated 350° oven about 40 minutes, or until the top springs back when touched.

Unmold onto a round plate and dust the top with a bit of powdered sugar if desired. May be served warm or cold.

SURPRISE DOUGHNUT HOLES

*Surprise your friends with the airy lightness of these little round dough-
nut balls. Like all doughnuts, these are best served hot, but they still
taste good cold.*

1 cup water	1/4 teaspoon salt
1/2 cup (1 stick) butter or	4 eggs
margarine	Oil for deep-fat frying
1 cup potato starch flour	Cinnamon sugar
1 tablespoon sugar	

In a 2-quart saucepan, heat water and butter until the mixture
boils. Remove pan from heat and stir in, all at once, the combined
flour, sugar, and salt. Continue stirring until the mixture forms a ball
and pulls away from the sides of the pan. Then, with an electric
mixer, beat in the eggs, one at a time, beating well after each addition.

Meanwhile, heat the oil for deep-fat frying. Use either an electric
skillet set at 375° or an automatic deep-fry kettle (such as a Fry-
Daddy). Use at least 1 inch of oil in the skillet or add oil up to the
marked line on an automatic fry kettle.

Drop the batter into the heated oil by small rounded teaspoonfuls,
a few at a time. Fry until they are golden brown, turning them to
brown evenly. They will puff up to about 1 1/2 inches as they cook
(about 5 minutes altogether). Remove and drain on paper towels.

While still warm, shake in a plastic bag with cinnamon sugar (2
tablespoons sugar to 1/2 teaspoon cinnamon). *Makes 3 dozen holes.*

DUTCH BABIES

An oven omelet with a texture between pancake and soufflé.

1/4 cup (1/2 stick) butter or margarine	1/2 cup milk or nondairy liquid
3 eggs	1/4 cup GF flour mix

Melt the butter in a glass pie pan in the oven. Meanwhile, mix eggs and milk in blender. Add flour and blend again. Pour into pie pan. Bake 18 minutes in preheated 425° oven. Serve with syrup, jam, or crushed fruit. *Makes 4 servings.*

VEGETABLE QUICHE WITH MASHED POTATO CRUST

In my first conversation with Dr. Winkelman, he praised his wife's gluten-free quiche. Jan Winkelman shares her recipe with us here.

Crust	1/2 cup grated Cheddar cheese
3 cups mashed potatoes seasoned with salt and pepper	1/2 cup mushrooms, sliced
1/3 cup minced onion	1/2 cup broccoli flowers
	1/4 cup sliced green pepper
Filling	1/2 cup grated carrots
1/2 cup grated Swiss cheese	3 eggs
	1 cup milk

Mix the seasoned mashed potatoes with minced onion and with them sculpt a shell in a buttered 9″ pie pan. Bake in preheated 350° oven for 15 minutes. (Leave oven on.)

Remove from oven and layer cheeses on the bottom, then add the vegetables. Fill the crust to slightly mounded. Beat together the eggs and milk and pour over all. Bake at 350° for 30 to 40 minutes or until you can cut through the quiche easily. *Makes 6 servings.*

VARIATION: Substitute other vegetables such as asparagus, celery, corn, and so on. For a nonvegetarian dish, add ham or cooked chicken.

VARIATION FOR THOSE ALLERGIC TO EGGS: You may substitute 1 package of Egg Beaters for the eggs and use only 7/8 cup milk.

VARIATION FOR A RICHER QUICHE: Use either eggs or Egg Beaters with 1 cup sour cream or nondairy substitute.

TOAD-IN-THE-HOLE

This meat and pastry dish may have been the original poor man's version of roast beef and Yorkshire pudding. A good brunch main dish, it goes well with curried fruit.

1 cup GF flour mix	1/2 teaspoon salt
2 eggs	Pepper to taste
1 cup milk or nondairy liquid	1 pound pork sausage links

In food processor or blender, combine flour, eggs, milk, salt, and pepper. Mix at high speed until well blended. Refrigerate for at least 1 hour.

Meanwhile, prick each sausage with a fork and place in a frying pan with 2 tablespoons water. Cook, covered, over low heat for 2 minutes. Raise heat to medium low, uncover, and cook, turning frequently, until sausages are well browned.

Cut sausages into approximately 1-inch pieces and lay in single layer in a greased 2-quart, flat casserole dish. Pour batter over them and bake in a preheated 400° oven for 30 minutes. Serve immediately. *Makes 4 to 6 servings.*

OVERNIGHT CASSEROLE

A hearty brunch or luncheon casserole that goes from the refrigerator to the oven, saving the busy hostess time in the morning to get ready for guests.

6 to 8 slices GF bread, crusts removed	6 eggs
6 slices Swiss cheese	2 cups milk or nondairy liquid
1 pound ground pork sausage*	Dash of salt

Line a 9″ × 13″ greased pan with enough bread to cover the bottom. Top with slices of Swiss cheese and the pork sausage, which has been cooked a little and drained.

Beat the eggs and add the milk and salt. Pour this mixture over the bread and refrigerate overnight. Bake the next morning in preheated 350° oven for 1 hour. *Makes 6 servings.*

*Ground turkey may be substituted for the pork sausage. Be sure to season the turkey well. I like a salt-free herb seasoning.

APPETIZERS AND SNACKS

Trying to snack from a party table is usually frustrating to a celiac or anyone else who must avoid wheat.

Some cheeses contain flavorings that are not gluten free, and many prepared meat slices contain wheat starch for a binder. Beware of dips that might contain gluten in their seasonings, and avoid any cream mixtures whose base is questionable. Crackers or buns will usually have a wheat flour base.

Thus, the celiac must stick to eating only the cheeses he or she is familiar with, the raw vegetables, the potato chips, and the wheat-free corn chips. (Some flavored chips may contain gluten in the seasoning.)

If you know you are going to attend a function where only appetizers and dips will be served, you might carry your own rice crackers, which you can find in the oriental section of most large grocery stores, or, if possible, suggest to the hostess that you make and bring one of the dishes. There are several packaged salad dressing mixes, such as Hidden Valley Ranch, that are gluten free and may be safely combined with mayonnaise and sour cream as a dip for raw vegetables or potato chips. For a dip lower in calories, replace the sour cream with cottage cheese. Any hostess would be happy to have this addition to her table.

I've included here a few more elaborate family favorites and some created by my friends when they were challenged by my diet.

I've also added a granola mix great for munching, as a cereal at breakfast, as a snack on a trail hike, or made up into bars by the recipe included.

CHEESE BALL

Purchased cheese balls are often made with a seasoning or filler containing gluten, so why not make your own? This simple recipe takes only a short time to prepare and can be made ahead of time and refrigerated.

1/2 cup grated Cheddar
cheese
One 8-ounce package
cream cheese
1/4 cup mayonnaise

1/2 cup minced onion
Dash of salt, or to taste
1/4 cup pecan meats, finely
chopped

Blend both cheeses, mayonnaise, onion, and salt. Shape into a ball and place in refrigerator until firm. Roll ball in nuts. Store in refrigerator. Serve with small rice crackers at the side and let people spread from the ball onto their crackers. *Makes a ball about 2 1/2 inches in diameter.*

SHRIMP CHEESE SPREAD

This hors d'oeuvre served hot from the broiler makes your guests think you've gone to a lot of trouble for them. But don't save it just for guests. Use it for late evening snacking or let it take the place of other munchies while watching afternoon games on television.

8 ounces sharp
cheese
One 4-ounce can shrimp,
drained
3 green onions
1/4 green pepper

One 8-ounce can ripe
olives, drained
1/2 cup (1 stick)
margarine, melted
One 8-ounce can tomato
sauce

Grind together or blend in food processor the cheese, shrimp, green onions, green pepper, and pitted olives. Then add the melted margarine and the tomato sauce.

Spread this mixture on GF buns or slices of GF bread. These may be cut into circles with a biscuit cutter or (as I prefer) into triangles, 2 or 4 to a slice, depending on how fancy your party. Put them under the broiler until the spread melts and bubbles. The mixture will keep several days in the refrigerator, and the buns or bread can be spread shortly ahead of time. *Makes approximately 1½ pints, serving 8 to 12.*

CHEESE STICKS

If you're tired of the same gluten-free crackers on the grocery shelves, try baking your own. These cheese sticks are great for parties, but they also taste good with soups, in lunches, or for just plain snacking. Their flavor varies with the strength of the cheese; I use medium Cheddar, but if you love sharp cheese, use that.

½ pound Cheddar cheese	⅛ teaspoon ground
2 tablespoons butter or	pepper
margarine	¾ cup rice flour
1 large egg	¼ cup potato starch flour
½ teaspoon salt	1 teaspoon xanthan gum

Grate the cheese (you should have approximately 2 cups). Set aside. Place butter in bowl of mixer and beat until creamy. Add egg, salt, and pepper. Beat until blended. Beat in cheese a third at a time, until combined. Stir in flours and xanthan gum until thoroughly blended. Work the dough into a ball. If dough doesn't stick together, add cold water 1 tablespoon at a time until a ball can be formed. Don't worry about overworking. The sticks can be firm.

Divide dough, rolling half at a time between sheets of wax paper or plastic wrap to form a 7-×-14-inch rectangle about ⅛ inch thick. Cut with pastry wheel into ½-×-7-inch strips and place on baking sheets. Bake in preheated 400° oven for 6 to 8 minutes, until deep golden.

Let cool on racks and store airtight up to 1 week. *Makes 56 cheese sticks.*

PUPS IN BLANKETS

Prepare pastry for Cheese Sticks, using medium-sharp Cheddar cheese. Roll out as described but cut into 1- × -4-inch bars. On each, place cut sections of small gluten-free hot dogs or cocktail sausages. Roll the pastry around the meat. Bake in preheated 400° oven for 6 to 8 minutes. These can be prepared ahead of time and popped into the oven just before serving. *Makes about 4 dozen pups in blankets.*

CHEESE PUFFS

This chou pastry is far easier to make than your guests will think. These tiny puffs will elicit raves. If you wish, you may use ½ cup potato starch flour and ½ cup rice flour instead of all potato starch flour.

4 ounces Cheddar cheese	⅛ teaspoon nutmeg
1 cup water	1 cup potato starch flour
½ cup (1 stick) margarine or butter	4 large eggs

Grate the cheese (you should have 1 cup). Set aside. Place water, margarine, and nutmeg in 2- to 3-quart saucepan. Bring to a full boil over medium heat. Turn off heat and add flour all at once, stirring until mixture leaves sides of pan and forms a ball. Remove from stove.

Add eggs, one at a time, beating well after each addition. Stir in ½ cup of the grated cheese. Drop the mixture by small spoonfuls on a greased baking sheet to make balls about 1½ inches in diameter. Sprinkle remaining cheese on puffs.

Bake in preheated 400° oven for 20 to 25 minutes, until golden brown. Remove baking sheet from oven. Prick the puffs with a fork and return to turned-off oven for 5 minutes to crisp. Serve warm. *Makes about 3 dozen puffs.*

MUSHROOM TARTS

These bite-sized appetizers can be made ahead and frozen to be pulled out and reheated in the microwave while the party is in progress. The compliments you get from guests will prove they are well worth the trouble.

PASTRY DOUGH

>3 ounces cream cheese, at room temperature
>1/2 cup (1 stick) butter or margarine
>1 cup GF flour mix

Cream together the cream cheese and butter. Add the flour and mix well with a fork or pastry cutter. The dough will form a ball.

Roll out the dough between sheets of plastic wrap dusted with rice flour. (It is easier to do this if you divide the dough into two or three sections.) Cut circles of pastry with a glass or a biscuit cutter and fit them into and up the sides of tartlet pans or small muffin tins. (You may prefer to work the dough into small balls and press with the fingers into and up the sides of the tins.) Chill.

FILLING

1/2 pound fresh mushrooms	1/2 teaspoon salt
1/4 cup fresh parsley	3/4 teaspoon ground marjoram
5 green onions	6 tablespoons grated Cheddar cheese
3 tablespoons butter or margarine	6 tablespoons GF bread crumbs
2 tablespoons vegetable oil	

Finely chop the mushrooms in the food processor. Remove them and mince the parsley. Remove the parsley and mince the green onions, using 2 to 3 inches of the green stem.

In a frying pan, heat the butter and oil. Add the minced vegetables and sauté over medium heat for about 6 minutes. The vegetables will start to give off their liquid and thicken a little. Transfer mixture to a bowl and add the salt, marjoram, grated cheese, and bread crumbs. Mix well.

Divide the filling among the chilled tart shells. Bake in preheated 350° oven for 20 to 25 minutes. Let cool for 5 minutes before unmolding. *Makes approximately 2 1/2 dozen small tartlets or 18 larger ones.*

To freeze, cool first and then wrap carefully. Reheat in microwave or in 375° oven for about 7 to 10 minutes. Serve hot.

QUICHE BITES: Instead of the mushroom filling, use half of the recipe for Crustless Seafood Quiche on page 174. The baking time is the same as for the mushroom tarts.

SWEDISH MEATBALLS

I live in a Scandinavian neighborhood and here no party is complete unless the table boasts at least one serving dish of these tiny, tasty meatballs.

1 1/2 pounds extra-lean ground beef
3/4 cup GF cereal, crushed, or GF bread crumbs
2 small eggs
2 tablespoons chili sauce
1 tablespoon instant minced onion
1 teaspoon salt
1/8 teaspoon pepper
1/2 teaspoon GF curry powder

Put all ingredients in a mixing bowl and knead together with hands until well mixed. Form into 1-inch balls and brown in a Teflon-coated or lightly oiled frying pan, turning or rolling them to get all sides crusty. Then place in a 9″ × 13″ baking pan and bake in preheated 350° oven for about 25 minutes.

You can make these a day ahead and warm them up to serve in a chafing dish with picks for eating. *Makes 2 dozen meatballs.*

GUACAMOLE DIP

This spirited avocado dip is a natural for our diet, for it goes best with Fritos or corn tortilla chips.

2 ripe avocados	$^1/_4$ teaspoon chili powder
1 tablespoon grated onion	$^1/_3$ cup mayonnaise
1 tablespoon lemon juice	Hot sauce or a salsa to
1 teaspoon salt	taste

Peel the avocados and mash in a bowl with a fork. Stir in the onion, lemon juice, salt, and chili powder. Blend in the mayonnaise. Add the hot sauce or a salsa to taste, depending on how hot you like it. Chill covered tightly with plastic wrap. Serve with corn or tortilla chips. *Makes approximately 1 cup dip.*

MICROWAVE CRAB DIP

For seafood lovers, a dip that spreads well on small rice crackers.

One 6-ounce can crab meat	$^1/_4$ cup minced onion
One 3-ounce package cream cheese, softened	1 tablespoon lemon juice
$^1/_2$ cup mayonnaise	$^1/_8$ teaspoon Tabasco sauce

Drain and flake the crab meat. Beat the softened cream cheese until smooth. Stir in mayonnaise, crab meat, onion, lemon juice, and Tabasco sauce. Spoon into a small microwave dish. Microwave at medium for 3 to 4 minutes until bubbly. If you prefer, bake in pre-heated 350° oven for 30 minutes. *Makes 1 cup dip.*

GRANOLA

I created this recipe originally as a gluten-free breakfast cereal for myself. I discovered it's great as a snack or in a survival packet on trips, and it is especially tasty made up into granola bars.

6 cups puffed rice
1 cup dry-roasted soy-
   beans
1 cup unsweetened flake
   coconut

1 cup sunflower seeds (if
   unsalted, add 1/2
   teaspoon salt)
1/4 cup honey
1/4 cup vegetable oil
2 cups raisins

Spray Pam in a large roaster. Put in the puffed rice, soybeans, coconut, and sunflower seeds.

In a saucepan combine the honey and oil and heat to boiling. Watch and stir constantly, as the mixture has a tendency to foam over the minute it comes to a boil. Remove from heat and drizzle this over the mixture in the roaster. Stir in well.

Bake in preheated 225° oven for 2 hours, stirring every 30 minutes to keep the mixture from sticking together. Then add raisins and turn off the oven. Put the pan back in the oven and let the granola cool down and dry out some. (This can easily be left overnight.) Store airtight in cans. *Makes 10 cups granola.*

NOTE: This basic recipe can be varied as your taste dictates. Replace raisins with other dried fruit, coconut with chopped nuts. Add pine nuts with the sunflower seeds. Try popped corn, chopped in a food processor, instead of all puffed rice. Add grated orange rind. The variety is endless.

GRANOLA BARS

Marvelous for lunches, travel, hiking, or just plain snacking. The preceding recipe for granola makes enough for plenty of breakfast cereal plus these bars, or two batches of bars.

1/2 cup brown sugar
1/4 cup dark corn syrup
1/3 cup sweetened condensed milk
2 tablespoons butter or margarine, melted
1/2 teaspoon vanilla
4 1/2 cups Granola, page 126, chopped in food processor
   to very coarse granules

Mix brown sugar, corn syrup, condensed milk, margarine, and vanilla together well. Pour over the granola and mix thoroughly. It will be sticky.

Butter your hands and flatten the mixture into a greased 9″ × 13″ pan. Bake in preheated 350° oven for 20 minutes.

Let cool about 10 minutes and cut into 1 1/2- × -3-inch bars. If you leave it longer, it will be hard to cut. *Makes 20 bars.*

Soups and Chowders

The day I was diagnosed and heard I would have to avoid gluten, I raced from the doctor's office to the store to find something quick to fix. I assumed soups would be safe. To my surprise, every can listed as an ingredient wheat flour or modified food starch. In desperation I grabbed a can of vegetable soup without the word *starch* on the label and hurried home to open it.

When I poured it into the pan, I saw, mixed in with the vegetable chunks, little round spots of barley—another of the forbidden gluten grains. I dumped the soup down the garbage disposal unit.

You have probably discovered, as I did, that most canned soups contain one of these three: barley, gluten for thickening, or pasta for body. And your hunger for soup is probably as keen as was mine when I poured out that vegetable soup.

Soups in a restaurant can also be poison for a celiac. Chowders and cream soups are invariably thickened with wheat flour, while poultry and vegetable soups will contain either noodles or barley, or both. Even powdered and dried soups must be suspect. They often contain wheat starch for thickening, although there are some that are gluten free. Some are available by mail (see pages 221–222) and a few can be found on the grocery shelves.

I've taken to making my own soups and freezing them in small quantities so I will never again go hungry for soup.

SOUPS FEATURING
VEGETABLES

QUICK VEGETABLE SOUP

If you're lucky enough to have a small pressure cooker, this soup can be made in minutes and tastes like the old-fashioned, long-simmered soup of yesterday.

If you don't, this soup can be simmered slowly with the same results. Using beef stock instead of some of the water will help the flavor, but remember to reduce the salt if the stock is salted.

1/4 pound lean ground beef	One 8-ounce can V8 juice
3 cups hot water	1/2 cup chopped cabbage
1/2 cup diced carrots	1 tablespoon chopped parsley
1/4 cup diced onion	1 teaspoon salt
1/2 cup sliced celery	1/8 teaspoon pepper

Brown the beef in the pressure cooker. Add the rest of the ingredients. Cover, set control at 15, and cook for 3 minutes after control jiggles. Remove from heat and let stand 5 minutes. Then reduce pressure by letting cold water run over pan. *Makes 4 servings.*

SAVORY MINESTRONE

Almost all the canned minestrone soups include pasta as one ingredient, thus they are forbidden to a celiac. You can make the following soup without pasta or add GF pasta either purchased or made from the recipe on page 150.

This is an excellent full-meal soup. The combination of sweet sausage, vegetables, and beans fills most of your nutritional requirements. It is so good the whole family will enjoy it.

1 pound Italian sweet
    sausage
1 tablespoon vegetable oil
1 cup diced onion
1 clove garlic, minced
1 cup diced carrots
1 teaspoon crumbled basil
2 small zucchini, sliced
One 16-ounce can
    tomatoes, undrained

Two 14½-ounce cans beef
    stock (see Note)
2 cups shredded cabbage
1 teaspoon salt
¼ teaspoon pepper
One 16-ounce can Great
    Northern beans,
    undrained
Optional: ¼ cup GF pasta

Slice sausage crosswise into ½-inch slices and brown in oil in a deep saucepan or Dutch oven. Add onion, garlic, carrots, and basil. Cook for 5 minutes. Add zucchini, tomatoes with their juice, beef stock, cabbage, salt, and pepper. Bring soup to boil; reduce heat and simmer, covered, for 1 hour. Add beans with their liquid and cook another 20 minutes. Add pasta if desired. This soup keeps well and tastes even better the next day. It also freezes well. *Makes 8 servings.*

NOTE: You may make the beef stock from gluten-free powdered beef bouillon. Follow the directions for 3½ cups stock. At this time Maggi and Crescent are two powdered bases that do not contain gluten.

DAISY'S HOMEMADE
TOMATO SOUP

Tomato soup from the market shelves usually contains some form of gluten, so during one summer of an abundant tomato harvest, I pulled out my mother's recipe for homemade tomato soup. This family recipe is easy to make and far better tasting than the canned soups.

I make this by the quart during tomato season when vine-ripened tomatoes are inexpensive and plentiful. Then I freeze the soup in 1-cup or 2-cup freezer containers for use all winter long. It can be eaten as a soup after thawing and heating with the addition of cream or a nondairy substitute, or it can be used in many recipes calling for tomatoes or tomato soup.

1 quart ripe tomatoes, quartered	1 tablespoon dried minced onion
1 tablespoon sugar	1/8 teaspoon tarragon
1/4 teaspoon salt	

Wash tomatoes and cut up into saucepan. Mash slightly so there is juice in the bottom of the pan. Add the sugar, salt, onion, and tarragon and bring to boil on medium or medium low heat. Be sure to stir so the tomatoes don't stick to the bottom of the pan. After they reach a boil, turn down heat and simmer until tomatoes are soft. I like to leave them at least an hour for all the seasonings to blend together.

Put mixture through a Foley food mill to eliminate the skins and most of the seeds. Let the soup cool before filling your freezer cartons. To serve, thaw, heat, and add a dash of cream or nondairy substitute. Don't heat after the cream is added, as it tends to curdle.

If you don't have a food mill, peel the tomatoes before cooking, then purée the cooked soup in a blender or food processor.

I usually make this in 2-quart batches to save time. Just double all ingredients. The double batch will make 6 cups of soup plus enough for a taste for yourself.

TOMATO CHEESE SOUP

In this soup the cheese is not cooked with the soup; it is put in the bowl and the broth poured over it, causing the cheese to turn to strings that trail from the spoon like the watches in a Dali painting.

2 teaspoons margarine or butter	1 1/2 cups chicken broth*
1 tablespoon chopped onion	1 tomato, peeled and chopped
1 small clove garlic, minced	Salt and pepper to taste
1 teaspoon chopped fresh cilantro (coriander)	1/2 cup shredded Monterey Jack cheese
	1/2 cup shredded Cheddar cheese

In small saucepan, melt margarine over medium heat; add onion and garlic and stir often until onion is clear. Stir in cilantro, broth, and tomato. Bring to a boil, cover, reduce heat, and simmer for about 10 minutes to blend flavors. Season to taste. (If broth is salted you may not need more salt.)

Place equal portions of jack and Cheddar cheeses in 2 large soup bowls. Ladle soup over cheese. *Makes 2 servings.*

This can easily be doubled or redoubled to serve 4 or 8.

*You may make your own stock from chicken backs and necks, use canned chicken broth, or use a powdered GF chicken soup base. For the latter, you use 1 teaspoon (or less) of base per cup of water.

CZECHOSLOVAKIAN CABBAGE SOUP

When my garage mechanic learned I was writing a cookbook, he gave me this favorite family recipe that he cooks up on his days off. After I tasted it, I begged permission to add it to the cookbook. This is not a quick-cooking soup, but one that tastes better for slow simmering—and even better heated up the next day.

This is a traditional country soup of Czechoslovakia. The beef bones, short ribs, vegetables, and seasonings make it hearty enough for a whole meal.

2 pounds beef soup bones
1 cup chopped onion
3 carrots, diced
2 cloves garlic, chopped
1 bay leaf
2 pounds beef short ribs
1 teaspoon dried thyme
1 teaspoon paprika
8 cups water
1 head cabbage, chopped
   (8 cups)

Two 16-ounce cans
   tomatoes, undrained
2 teaspoons salt
1/2 teaspoon Tabasco
   sauce
1/2 cup chopped parsley
3 tablespoons lemon juice
3 tablespoons sugar
One 16-ounce can
   sauerkraut, drained

Place beef bones, onion, carrots, garlic, and bay leaf in a roasting pan. Top with short ribs and sprinkle with thyme and paprika. Roast uncovered in preheated 450° oven for 20 minutes, until meat is browned.

Transfer meat and vegetables to a large kettle. Add water, cabbage, tomatoes and their liquid, salt, and Tabasco. Bring to a boil. Cover and simmer 1 1/2 hours. Skim off fat.

Add parsley, lemon juice, sugar, and sauerkraut. Cook, uncovered, for 1 hour. Remove bones and short ribs from kettle. Trim meat from bones, cut into cubes, and return to the soup. Cook 5 minutes longer.

This will make 12 servings, but none ever goes to waste since it freezes well.

PUMPKIN SOUP

The special flavor in this soup comes from peanut butter. It sounds weird but tastes delicious. This recipe serves two, but it can be doubled or redoubled to serve a crowd.

1 tablespoon unsalted butter	1/4 cup peanut butter
1 cup pumpkin pie filling	1 1/2 cups chicken or turkey broth
1/2 cup puréed sweet potatoes	1/4 teaspoon pepper
	1/4 teaspoon salt

Melt butter in saucepan over medium heat. Stir in pumpkin, sweet potatoes, and peanut butter.

Add broth, pepper, and salt if desired (you may not need salt if the broth is salted). Reduce heat and simmer for 20 minutes.

Serve garnished, if you like, with a dab of sour cream or nondairy substitute sprinkled with chopped chives. *Makes 2 servings.*

POTATO LEEK SOUP

A hearty soup that reminds one of a warm kitchen on a cold winter evening. Serve with warm bread, muffins, or biscuits for a full meal.

3 fist-sized potatoes	3/4 teaspoon salt
3 leeks	1/2 cup water
1 stalk celery	3 cups milk or nondairy liquid
1 large carrot	Snippets of thyme, marjoram, and basil
1/4 cup (1/2 stick) butter or margarine	

Peel and cube the potatoes, clean and chop the leeks, chop the celery, and peel and dice the carrot. Place the prepared vegetables and the butter in a saucepan. Add the salt and cook over medium heat, stirring constantly, until butter is melted and the vegetables are coated.

Add the water and bring to a boil, then cover and simmer. Cook until the potatoes are tender, adding more water if needed.

Remove vegetables and purée with the milk in a food processor or blender. Return to saucepan and add herbs. Reheat but do not boil. *Makes 6 1/2 cups, 6 servings.*

NOTE: If green stalks of the leeks are used, the soup will be green; if only the white part, the soup will be creamy white. Good either way.

MICROWAVE POTATO SOUP

I think of potato soup as a hearty cold-weather dish. This is quick and easy for the working man or woman to fix.

1 slice bacon, diced	1 cup chicken broth
1 medium-sized potato	1 cup milk or nondairy
1/8 teaspoon dried	liquid
thyme	Dash of pepper

Place bacon in 1- to 1 1/2-quart glass bowl. Cover and microwave on high until bacon is brown, 1 to 1 1/2 minutes. Lift out bacon and drain on a paper towel.

Discard half the drippings. Peel and dice the potato and add with thyme to the remaining drippings. Cook on high until potato is tender, 4 to 6 minutes.

Mash the potato with a fork. Stir in broth and milk. Cover and cook on high, stirring once or twice, until steaming, 4 to 5 minutes. Season with pepper to taste and sprinkle with the bacon. *Makes 2 servings.*

SOUPS WITH CLAMS
OR CHICKEN

NEW ENGLAND
CLAM CHOWDER

Canned clam chowders are usually thickened with wheat starch. There is no need for this, as the potatoes in the chowder provide enough thickening. This recipe is quick to fix and filling enough for a main dish at lunch or supper.

1 medium onion	1 cup nondairy liquid or
2 slices bacon	evaporated milk
1 cup peeled and diced raw	1 cup water
potatoes	Pepper to taste
One 6 1/2-ounce can	1/2 teaspoon salt
chopped clams	Optional: 3 or 4
2 cups chicken	tablespoons grated
stock	carrot for garnish

Chop the onion; mince the bacon. Fry bacon gently until cooked but not crisp. Then add onions. Sauté until onions are clear.

Meanwhile dice potatoes. Drain the clams, reserving the juice. Transfer the bacon and onion to a soup pan and add the potatoes, clam juice, and chicken stock. Cook until potatoes are tender.

Place half the mixture in blender and blend until smooth. Return blended mixture to saucepan and add clams, nondairy liquid or evaporated milk, water, pepper, and salt. (If the chicken stock is salted you may not need salt.) Heat and serve. If desired, just before serving add the grated carrot and cook a minute or two. The carrot adds color and texture to the soup. *Makes 1 1/2 quarts, 6 to 8 servings.*

NOTE: You may leave the potatoes diced instead of blending them. In this case, thicken the soup with a thin paste of potato starch and water. Start with 2 tablespoons and let cook before adding more, as the potato starch thickens about twice as much liquid as wheat flour paste. I cannot give an exact amount of starch, since potatoes have different thickening properties and people prefer different consistencies of chowder.

CLAM CORN CHOWDER: Add one 8-ounce can creamed corn to the clam chowder recipe before the chowder is thickened (the corn may change the consistency). The chowder may not need thickening. Be sure the corn is gluten free.

CHINESE CORN SOUP

This is a quick corn and chicken soup that makes a full meal. I clipped it from the newspaper and assumed it was an Americanized version of a Chinese dish until I was served this in China and discovered that my soup tasted exactly like that served in the Chinese restaurant in Canton.

This recipe can be found in Enjoy Chinese Cuisine, *by Judy Lew, to whom the recipe was credited in the* Seattle Times.

2 whole chicken breasts, boned and skinned	1 teaspoon salt
1 egg white	1 1/2 teaspoons pepper
1 tablespoon rice wine	1 egg, beaten
1 tablespoon cornstarch	2 tablespoons cornstarch dissolved in 2
1 quart chicken stock	tablespoons water
One 8-ounce can creamed corn	

Dice the chicken breast into bite-sized pieces or slice to thin slivers and combine with the egg white, rice wine, and cornstarch. Set aside.

Bring to a boil the chicken stock, creamed corn, salt, and pepper. (If the chicken stock is already salted, you will need to reduce the salt here. I use none until it is ready for the table and then salt to taste.) When stock reaches a boil, add the chicken pieces, stirring constantly to break up chicken. Cook 1 minute.

Add the beaten egg in a thin stream, stirring slowly in one direction.

Thicken the soup with cornstarch and water mixture, stirring for a few minutes. *Makes 6 to 8 servings*, depending on whether you use as a full meal or a soup course.

HEARTY CHICKEN
NOODLE SOUP

The noodles used in canned soups contain gluten so, if you like noodles, you will have to make your own soups and add the GF products. You may use pure rice noodles or bean threads found in the oriental section of grocery stores, or make your own from the pasta recipe on page 150.

This hearty soup is a full meal at lunch and is excellent for the luncheon thermos, even better if the worker has access to a microwave.

3 cups chicken stock	2 tablespoons butter or
1/2 cup chopped celery	margarine
2/3 cup leftover cooked	2 tablespoons rice flour
chicken or one 4- or 6-	Salt to taste
ounce can chicken	1 tablespoon parsley flakes
1/2 cup diced carrots	Optional: 1/2 cup cream or
1/2 cup uncooked noodles	nondairy substitute

Simmer chicken stock, celery, chicken, and carrots until vegetables are tender, about 20 minutes. Add noodles and cook until they are done. (Bean threads take only a minute or two; rice noodles must be tested for doneness; homemade noodles take about 15 to 20 minutes.)

Melt butter and mix with the rice flour, adding a small amount of the hot chicken stock. Stir this mixture into the simmering soup. Add salt and parsley flakes.

Heat the cream (or nondairy substitute) if using, and add. The cream lightens the color of the soup. Let cook for short while. Do not boil after adding the cream. *Makes 5 or 6 servings.*

CREAM SOUPS

CREAM OF CHICKEN SOUP

Before I discovered I was a celiac, I used canned cream of chicken soup in many casseroles. When I found that all of those on the market are thickened with some form of gluten, I started making my own and freezing it in 1-cup portions for later use alone or in casseroles.

3 cups chicken stock	2 tablespoons sweet rice flour
1/2 cup finely chopped celery	1/2 cup cream or nondairy substitute
1/2 cup cubed cooked chicken	1 tablespoon minced parsley
2 tablespoons butter or margarine	Salt to taste
	Paprika, if desired

Simmer chicken stock, celery, and chicken until celery is tender.

Melt butter and blend in the sweet rice flour, adding a small amount of the chicken stock. Stir this mixture into the simmering stock.

Heat the cream (or nondairy substitute) and add this plus the seasonings. Let cook for short while. Do not boil after adding the cream. *Makes about 5 cups soup.*

CREAM OF MUSHROOM SOUP

A great soup for eating or for use in casseroles.

1/4 pound fresh mushrooms, chopped	2 cups cream or nondairy substitute
1/4 cup diced onion	2 tablespoons butter
1/2 cup sliced celery	2 tablespoons sweet rice flour
2 cups water or stock	Salt and pepper to taste

Place the vegetables in a saucepan with the stock and simmer, covered, for 20 minutes. Cool slightly and remove vegetables to food processor. Process briefly and return to stock.

Melt butter in a separate saucepan, add sweet rice flour, and stir until smooth. Mix the cream into the stock and pour slowly into butter-flour mixture. Cook, stirring constantly, until soup boils. Season to taste if the stock is unsalted. *Makes 4 1/2 cups soup.*

MICROWAVE CREAM OF BROCCOLI SOUP

For this I use 1 cup of the soup recipe on page 142, but you may prefer to use one of the gluten-free dried chicken soups.

2 cups chopped celery	2 cups milk or nondairy liquid
1 cup chopped onion	1 cup GF cream of chicken soup
One 10-ounce package frozen chopped broccoli	1/2 teaspoon salt, if desired
1 cup cottage cheese	1/8 teaspoon pepper

Cook celery, onion, and broccoli in 2 1/2-quart covered casserole in microwave on high for 6 minutes, stirring after 3 minutes. Set aside.

Blend cottage cheese in blender or food processor until very smooth; slowly add milk while continuing to blend. Add chicken soup to this mixture and blend again. Add the liquids to the vegetables. Microwave on high until heated through, about 3 minutes, without boiling. Add salt and pepper to taste. *Makes 6 servings.*

SOUPS CONTAINING BEANS, PEAS, OR LENTILS

Bean, pea, and lentil soups do not need thickeners but, surprisingly, a large number of commercial canners have added wheat flour to their products, thus forcing us to read labels carefully or to make our own.

They require little work but a long time on the stove, and all the recipes I've found make a large batch. If you can keep the rest of the family from taking too many second helpings, you will have enough left from the next three recipes to freeze for later use.

SPLIT PEA SOUP

This soup is so thick and hearty that it makes a full meal. And, since split peas are high in fiber, its food value is as great as the soup tastes.

1 ham hock	2 cloves garlic, minced
7 1/2 cups water	1 carrot, diced
2 1/2 cups dried split peas	1 teaspoon salt, or to taste
1 cup chopped onion	1/2 teaspoon pepper

Cook ham hock with water in covered soup kettle for 1 hour. Remove meat from bone and skin. Chop meat and put it back into water with the rest of the ingredients.

Simmer 40 minutes or more until soup is of desired consistency. (I simmer it several hours, until it becomes thick.) This freezes well. *Makes 8 cups.*

LENTIL SOUP

Another hearty soup that freezes well. Since lentils contain vitamin E, which we miss in our avoidance of wheat, and also calcium, which many celiacs lose in avoidance of milk products, they are a good substitute.

2 cups lentils	1 clove garlic, minced
2 quarts hot water	2 cloves
1 stalk celery, with leaves, chopped	1/2 teaspoon oregano, crushed
1 medium onion, chopped	Salt and pepper to taste
3 slices bacon, diced	

Cover lentils with hot water. There is no need to soak lentils. Add the celery, onion, bacon, garlic, cloves, and oregano to the lentils and place over high heat to bring to boil. Immediately reduce heat to simmer and cook for 2 1/2 to 3 hours, or until lentils are tender.

Remove the cloves. Add salt and pepper to taste (about 2 teaspoons salt and 1/8 teaspoon pepper) and serve or freeze. *Makes 6 to 8 servings.*

NOTE: To add flavor, substitute one 6-ounce can V8 juice for 3/4 cup of the water.

HILLBILLY SOUP (16-Bean Soup)

This is an original Ozark recipe that calls for many kinds of beans. Don't worry if you can't find them all; any combination of some of these beans is fine. I buy the lot and then make up small plastic bags of 1 1/2 cups each to cook later. Some I package with the recipe for gifts. Warning: Some health food stores are selling these packages with barley as one of the ingredients. Read the ingredient list.

Red kidney beans	Large white butter beans
Black-eyed peas	Speckled limas
Garbanzo beans	Field peas
Green split peas	Lentils
Yellow split peas	Pinto beans
Large navy beans	Black beans
Baby limas	Pink beans
Small navy beans	Small red beans

Wash 1 1/2 cups bean mixture. Cover with water, add 1 tablespoon salt, and soak overnight. Drain.

Put soaked beans in 2 quarts water. (For added flavor, substitute one 6-ounce can V8 juice for 3/4 cup of the water.) Add:

1/2 pound ham pieces	Salt and pepper to taste
1 clove garlic, chopped	1 onion, chopped
One 28-ounce can tomatoes	Optional: 1 green or red pepper, chopped
Juice of 1 lemon	

Bring to a simmer and let cook on low at least 4 hours. Check occasionally for liquid. As it cooks down it thickens. You can add water or not as you desire. I like the thicker soup and cook mine most of the day. The flavor improves with age. *Makes 8 to 10 servings.*

PASTA AND PIZZA

There is no more need for the celiac to watch other people eat pasta while he or she pushes rice around under the spaghetti sauce. I know it's not the same, for I tried that before I discovered that some dietary food companies produce gluten-free spaghetti, macaroni, and other pastas. (See pages 221–222 for listing.) You can also purchase rice noodles and bean threads in the oriental section of most grocery stores. Corn pastas can be found in some supermarkets and health food stores. Although these are blander than homemade pasta, they will satisfy a pasta craving, especially if you cook the pasta in a beef-flavored stock or flavor it with a lot of cheese.

But other pasta dishes, such as lasagne, stroganoff, and chicken and noodles, seem to need old-fashioned, homemade egg noodles. I finally developed a recipe using gluten-free flours that satisfies my taste in these dishes—and also that of my nonceliac pasta-loving friends. The pasta in the following recipes works well in a pasta machine, but you don't have to have one, even for ravioli. I give directions for making all the pastas without a machine. If you have one, follow the manufacturer's directions.

As for pizza, you don't have to curb your desire for that dish. I include recipes for four tasty crusts. Just use your imagination on the topping and have pizza anytime you crave it.

PASTA AND PASTA DISHES

HOMEMADE PASTA

The following pasta is the result of much experimentation. The mixture of the many flours plus the xanthan gum seems to be the secret of success. This makes a small recipe, so you can use it immediately or freeze the uncooked pasta to be used later. Drying isn't successful except for the smaller forms, such as salad macaroni. I keep the dried forms in my refrigerator. The recipe may be doubled and worked in 2 balls instead of 1 for more servings.

$^1/_3$ cup tapioca flour	$^1/_2$ teaspoon salt
$^1/_3$ cup cornstarch	1 tablespoon xanthan gum
2 tablespoons potato starch flour	2 large eggs
	1 tablespoon vegetable oil

Combine flours, salt, and xanthan gum. Beat eggs lightly and add oil. Pour egg into flour mixture and stir. This will feel much like pastry dough. Work together into a firm ball. Knead a minute or two.

Place ball of dough on your bread board and roll *as thin as possible.* One pasta book suggests you should be able to see the board through the dough. The dough is tough and, although almost transparent, will still handle well. Slice the noodles into very thin strips or, if using for lasagne, into $1^1/_2$- × -4-inch rectangles. The pasta is now ready to cook, or to freeze uncooked for later use.

Cook the pasta in salted boiling water to which 1 tablespoon of oil has been added for 10 to 20 minutes depending on the thickness and the size of your pieces. You will have to test for doneness. *Makes 3 servings as noodles alone, 5 to 6 servings in a mixed casserole.*

After years of abstinence, probably the first thing you will want to do is eat the noodles hot from the pan, slathered with butter and grated Parmesan cheese.

Use this pasta in all the following pasta recipes, whether cut in thin noodles, wide lasagne strips, spaghetti, or even in the ravioli recipe.

SPAGHETTI: Use the spaghetti cutter on your pasta machine. If you don't have a pasta machine, roll the dough very thin and cut your spaghetti as narrow as possible. This may turn out a bit uneven, but no one will notice when it is hidden under spaghetti sauce. Cook for 10 minutes in boiling salted water to which a tablespoon of oil has been added.

CHOW MEIN NOODLES: Make the pasta and cut as if for spaghetti. Then cut these strips into 1- to 1 1/2-inch pieces. Drop uncooked into hot oil and cook for a few seconds (they will probably take less than a minute). Remove from oil and drain on paper towels. Then use immediately or freeze. *Makes about 5 to 6 cups chow mein noodles.*

GREEN PASTA MADE
WITH BROCCOLI

This is similar to pasta made with spinach; I think it has a better flavor.

1/4 cup cooked broccoli	1/2 teaspoon salt
1/3 cup tapioca flour	1 tablespoon xanthan gum
1/3 cup cornstarch	2 large eggs
1/4 cup potato starch flour	1 tablespoon vegetable oil

Pat the broccoli as dry as possible with paper toweling. Purée it in blender.

Combine the flours (reserving 1 tablespoon of the potato starch flour), salt, and xanthan gum. Stir in the broccoli. Beat eggs and oil together. Add to the flours and work into a firm ball. Add the extra tablespoon of potato starch flour if needed to make the dough dry enough to handle and roll out.

Place ball of dough on board and roll out as thin as possible. Cut the noodles into thin strips. You are now ready to cook these or freeze them for later use.

Suggestions for serving: Boil the noodles in salted water until done. Drain, but leave them in the saucepan on stove turned to low. Add 2 tablespoons butter, about 1/4 cup cream, and 3/4 cup grated Cheddar cheese. Stir until the cheese melts. Swirl onto an oval platter. *Makes 3 or 4 servings.*

FETTUCCINE

This is a light version of fettuccine.

1 recipe Homemade Pasta,
  page 150, cut into
  1/8-inch strips
1/4 cup ricotta cheese
1/4 cup plain yogurt

1/4 cup grated Parmesan
  cheese
1 tablespoon margarine
Dash of black pepper

Cook the pasta in salted water. Drain well and return to the cooking pot. Add the ricotta cheese, yogurt, Parmesan cheese, margarine, and pepper and toss well to mix.

Transfer to a warm platter and serve. *Makes 3 servings.*

PASTA PROVOLONE

A richer, cheesier dish than the preceding one.

1 recipe Homemade Pasta,
    page 150, cut in thin
    strips
1 1/2 cups grated Monterey
    Jack cheese
1 cup grated provolone
    cheese
1/2 cup cream or nondairy
    substitute

1 cup sliced pitted ripe
    olives
1 tomato, cut in thin
    wedges
2 tablespoons dried
    basil
1/4 cup pine nuts

In a large saucepan, cook pasta. Drain and return pasta to the dry
pan. Add the cheeses and cream and heat, stirring to melt the cheese.
Stir in the olives, tomato, basil, and pine nuts. Heat through and
serve immediately. *Makes 4 or 5 servings.*

HAM AND CHICKEN PASTA

Another of those melt-in-the-mouth noodle dishes, my favorite.

1 recipe Homemade Pasta,
    page 150, cut into
    1/8-inch strips
4 egg yolks
1 cup cream or nondairy
    substitute
4 tablespoons (1/2 stick)
    butter

1/2 cup chicken or turkey
    strips
1/2 cup ham strips
Salt and pepper to
    taste
1 cup grated Parmesan
    cheese

Cook the pasta and drain.
In a small bowl, blend egg yolks and cream together.
Place butter in skillet and melt. Add turkey and ham to brown

lightly, then add the cooked pasta. Heat through. Add the egg yolks and cream and gently fold in until all is well mixed. Season to taste with salt and pepper before stirring in the grated cheese.

Serve immediately. *Makes 4 or 5 servings.*

MEAT SAUCE FOR SPAGHETTI

This is a rich, tasty sauce.

1 pound lean ground beef
1/4 cup chopped onion
2 cloves garlic, minced
1/4 cup chopped parsley
1/4 teaspoon basil
1/4 teaspoon thyme
1/4 teaspoon marjoram
One 8-ounce can sliced
  mushrooms

One 16-ounce can
  tomatoes
Two 8-ounce cans tomato
  sauce
Pinch each allspice, cloves,
  and nutmeg
1/2 teaspoon salt
Pepper to taste

Cook meat until brown with onion and garlic. Add chopped parsley, basil, thyme, marjoram, mushrooms, canned tomatoes, and tomato sauce. Add spices and salt and pepper. Bring to boil, turn down heat, and simmer for at least 2 hours. Serve over GF spaghetti. *Makes 6 servings.*

EASY VARIATION: Many of the commercial spaghetti sauces on the market are gluten free, so you can use them as they come from the jar or you can brown 1 pound of lean ground beef and 1 diced onion in skillet, add salt and pepper to taste, and then pour in 1 jar (approximately 26 ounces) of your favorite GF spaghetti sauce. Bring to boil, turn down heat, cover, and let simmer for 2 hours for the flavors to meld. Serve over cooked GF spaghetti and top, if desired, with grated Parmesan cheese.

THREE-CHEESE LASAGNE

Lasagne so good that when I took this to a lasagne party my dish was the first one emptied. I cut lasagne noodles with a pastry cutter to give a slightly wavy edge to the pasta.

1 recipe Homemade Pasta, page 150, cut into 1 1/2- × -4-inch rectangles
1 pound extra-lean ground beef
12 ounces mozzarella cheese
4 ounces Cheddar cheese
1 egg
One 16-ounce carton ricotta cheese
One 16-ounce jar GF spaghetti sauce

While the pasta is cooking in salted water with a bit of oil added, brown the meat in a heavy frying pan, and grate the mozzarella and Cheddar cheeses. Add the egg to the ricotta and blend together.

Now assemble the ingredients in a shallow casserole approximately 9″ × 13″. Pour a little sauce on the bottom, and on it place a layer of cooked noodles, using one-third of your noodles. Over this spread half the ricotta mixture, half the meat, and half the mozzarella. Spread on about a third of the sauce. Layer another row of pasta and repeat. Top with pasta, the remaining sauce, and the grated Cheddar cheese.

Bake in a preheated 350° oven until the sauce bubbles around the edges, about 1/2 hour.

This can be made ahead and baked just before serving or it can be frozen before or after baking. I usually make two casseroles and we eat one fresh; I freeze the other unbaked for another meal. If you store it, frozen or unfrozen, cover it with plastic wrap, not aluminum foil. Foil can react with the tomato sauce, shedding gray flakes over the lasagne. This makes enough to serve 6 to 10, depending on how much else will be served with it.

VEGETARIAN LASAGNE: Omit the meat and increase the Cheddar to 12 ounces. Mix the Cheddar with the mozzarella as you make the layers. If you wish, you may sauté about 1 cup of sliced mushrooms in butter and add them to the layers.

MOCK LASAGNE: Here is a lasagne without noodles, using, instead, one package (6 to 8) thick corn tortillas. Slice the tortillas into strips about 1 1/2 inches wide and layer with the remaining ingredients from either of the two preceding lasagne recipes. If you bake it immediately, the lasagne will have a mild corn taste. But if this is frozen and later thawed and baked, the flavor will be more like that of conventional lasagne.

THREE-CHEESE RAVIOLI

This simple three-cheese filling is one of the easiest to make and handle. This makes enough for a triple batch of pasta.

3/4 cup ricotta cheese	Salt and pepper to taste
2 tablespoons grated sharp Cheddar	1 small egg plus 1 egg reserved for wash
2 tablespoons grated mozzarella	Triple recipe Homemade Pasta, page 150

Blend cheeses, salt and pepper, and 1 egg in food processor until creamy.

Prepare the pasta. If you have a pasta machine with the ravioli attachment, follow directions for filling and cutting. If you have the inexpensive ravioli tray, follow directions for using it.

If you have neither, roll the sheet of pasta out to about 12 × 14 inches. Paint one side with a wash of beaten egg mixed with a little water. Onto this, drop the cheese filling in dabs less than 1/2 inch in size from the tip of a teaspoon. They should be about 2 to 2 1/4 inches apart. When the side is filled, fold the dough over and, with fingers or a rounded spoon handle, seal the dough between the small mounds. Cut with a pastry cutter or use a product called Krimpkut Sealer specially made for cutting and sealing at the same time. You should work quickly so the egg wash stays moist to help the pasta seal. Repeat with remaining pasta. When the ravioli are all made, either cook immediately in a large pot of boiling, salted water for 15 minutes (test for doneness) or freeze for later use. *Makes about 90 ravioli, or 10 to 12 servings.*

These are excellent served with a meat sauce (page 154).

CHICKEN RAVIOLI

A delicately flavored ravioli in a creamy white sauce, different and good.

Filling	Sauce
1/4 cup cooked broccoli	4 tablespoons (1/2 stick)
3/4 cup cooked chicken	butter
2 tablespoons grated	2 tablespoons sweet rice
Cheddar cheese	flour
Salt and pepper to taste	2 cups cream or nondairy
1 small egg	substitute
2 or 3 tablespoons chicken	1/3 teaspoon nutmeg
broth	Dash of pepper
	2/3 cup grated Cheddar
Triple recipe Homemade	cheese
Pasta, page 150	

Put all filling ingredients except the chicken broth in the blender or food processor. Blend them. Add the chicken broth a little at a time, blending after each addition, until filling has a creamy consistency.

Make a triple batch of pasta and follow the directions on page 156 for completing the ravioli. Freeze for later use or cook for 15 minutes in salted water. Test for doneness. Serve hot with the sauce.

Melt the butter in a 2-quart saucepan on medium low heat. Add the rice flour, stir, and slowly add the cream, continuing to stir so it doesn't lump. Add the nutmeg and pepper and continue to stir as the sauce thickens slightly. Add the cheese and blend in until it melts. The sauce is now ready to serve. Either put the ravioli into the sauce or pour the sauce over the hot ravioli in the serving dish. (I like to use a large low dish.) Sprinkle the top with nutmeg or paprika. *Makes 12 servings.*

CHICKEN NOODLE CASSEROLE

An old favorite with a new taste.

One 3-pound chicken	2 tablespoons sweet rice
1 recipe Homemade Pasta,	flour
page 150, cut into	1 teaspoon poultry
1/4-inch strips	seasoning
One 3-ounce package	3 green onions, sliced thin
cream cheese	One 8-ounce can water
1 cup sour cream	chestnuts, drained and
or nondairy	sliced
substitute	4 ounces sliced almonds

Wash and cut up the chicken and cook, covered, in 2 cups salted water until tender. Let cool in the broth. Skin, bone, and cut up chicken into slivers or chunks the size you prefer. Save the broth.

Make pasta, cut, and cook. If you add 2 tablespoons of powdered chicken soup base to the noodle water, the noodles will have more flavor. Drain and rinse pasta.

Place chicken and noodles in large casserole. Blend the cream cheese with the sour cream and rice flour and thin with 3/4 cup of the reserved chicken broth. Stir in the poultry seasoning, green onions, and water chestnuts. Spread this mixture over the chicken and noodles. (You may fold the sliced almonds into the mixture or scatter them on top of the assembled casserole.)

Bake in preheated 350° oven for 45 to 50 minutes. *Makes 6 servings.*

TUNA-CASHEW CASSEROLE

I pulled this old standby out of my recipe file and found it excellent with chow mein noodles.

1 1/2 cups Mushroom
    Sauce, page 186
1 cup milk or nondairy
    liquid
3 1/2 cups cooked
    Chow Mein Noodles,
    page 151

One 6 1/2-ounce can tuna
    fish
1/3 cup cashew nuts
1 cup celery, diced
1/4 cup minced onion
Dash of pepper
Salt to taste

Mix mushroom sauce and milk and pour over the remaining ingredients, which have been placed in a 2-quart casserole. Stir together to moisten thoroughly. Bake 50 to 60 minutes in preheated 325° oven. *Makes 6 to 8 servings.*

BEEF STROGANOFF

For years I envied my husband being able to order beef stroganoff in restaurants while I could only watch him eat it. After I created the recipe for homemade pasta, I worked on the stroganoff recipe and came up with this easy, excellent dish. I make the pasta and let it dry a bit while preparing the sauce. Then, after adding the sour cream, I cook the pasta while the sauce is heating.

1 pound beef sirloin
3 tablespoons rice flour
1/2 teaspoon salt
2 tablespoons vegetable oil
One 3-ounce can sliced
    mushrooms, or 1/2 cup
    sliced fresh mushrooms
1 cup chopped onion
1 clove garlic, minced
1 tablespoon catsup

1 can beef broth, or
    1 1/4 cups instant beef
    stock*
1 cup sour cream or
    nondairy substitute
2 tablespoons rice wine or
    dry white wine
1 recipe Homemade Pasta,
    page 150, cut into
    noodles

*You can use Crescent soup base or Romanoff MBT instant beef broth, but always read labels to confirm that these are still gluten free.

Cut beef into 1/4-inch strips. Combine 1 tablespoon flour and salt and coat meat. Heat skillet, add oil, and drop in coated meat. Brown quickly. Add drained canned or sliced fresh mushrooms, onion, and garlic. Cook 3 or 4 minutes until onion is crisp but tender.

Remove meat and mushrooms from pan. Add a bit more oil to pan drippings and blend in 2 remaining tablespoons rice flour. Put catsup in beef broth and stir into pan. Cook, stirring, over medium heat until thickened and bubbly.

Return browned meat and mushrooms to skillet. Stir in sour cream or nondairy substitute and wine. Cook slowly until heated through. Do not boil. Keep warm over hot water while you cook the pasta. Serve sauce over hot buttered noodles. *Makes 4 or 5 servings.*

PIZZAS

PAT'S THIN YEAST CRUST

Pat Garst, author of Gluten-Free Cooking, *shares this recipe for a thin yeast crust for pizza. This is easy to make, with great flavor.*

1 1/2 teaspoons instant dry
   yeast granules
About 1 cup warm water,
   105° to 115°
1 teaspoon sugar
2/3 cup rice flour

1/3 cup potato starch flour
1 tablespoon potato flour
1 1/2 teaspoons melted
   shortening
1 teaspoon salt

In mixing bowl, dissolve the yeast in 1/2 cup of the warm water with the sugar added. Let set until yeast bubbles and the quantity doubles.

Add all the rest of the ingredients, using enough of the remaining water to get a dough the consistency of cake frosting that will spread, not run, when all ingredients are thoroughly beaten. Grease a

10″ × 15″ jelly roll pan. Pour batter down center and spread with a spatula. Run a teaspoon around edges, forcing batter up the sides.

If you prefer, you may do as I do and pour the batter and spread in a circle on the pan, forming a 12- to 12½-inch circle with raised edges. The batter handles well and will make a circle shape easily. Leave more at edges for raised sides.

Add sauce and toppings (see page 164). Bake in preheated 425° oven for 25 to 30 minutes. *Makes 6 servings.*

JILL'S QUICK AND EASY PIZZA CRUST

Jill Ryan of Seattle's Gluten Intolerance Group claims she never makes anything unless it can be quick and easy. This is especially true for her excellent pizza crust recipe.

¹/₄ cup milk	Optional: ¹/₄ teaspoon
2 large eggs	xanthan gum
¹/₃ cup cornstarch	1 teaspoon salt
²/₃ cup rice flour	¹/₄ cup shortening, melted

Beat the milk and eggs together. Add the flours, xanthan gum (if used), and salt. Mix in melted shortening.

Spread into greased 9″ × 13″ pan or (as I do) spread with a spatula in a 12-inch circle about ¹/₄ inch thick on cookie sheet or round pizza pan, leaving a thicker crust around the outside of the circle to keep the sauce and cheese from running over onto the pan.

Spread sauce evenly over the unbaked crust and top with your favorite toppings (see page 164). Bake in preheated 400° oven for about 25 minutes. *Makes 6 servings.*

THICK YEAST-FREE
PIZZA CRUST

For a thicker pizza crust, try this easy recipe, which requires no rising but tastes like a yeast bread crust.

1 cup potato starch flour	1 tablespoon baking powder
1/2 cup cornstarch	1/2 teaspoon salt
1/2 cup tapioca flour	2 tablespoons shortening
1/2 cup dry milk powder	3/4 cup water

In a mixing bowl, place the flours, dry milk, baking powder, and salt. Cut in the shortening, rubbing with the fingers until it feels like cornmeal. Pour in the water and stir until the dough clings together in a ball. Work with the hands, kneading the dough until smooth. Form into 2 balls.

Place a ball on the center of a greased cookie sheet or pizza tin and, covering it with plastic wrap, press it out into a 10-inch circle about 1/4 inch thick except at the edges, which should be about 1/2 inch thick to contain the sauce and fillings. Repeat with the second ball. Fill with desired sauce and toppings (see page 164). Bake in preheated 400° oven for 20 to 22 minutes.

To freeze one of the pizzas, place it on a prepared, foil-covered cardboard circle and fill as above. Wrap securely with plastic wrap, then foil, and place in freezer. To cook, slide from the wrappings to the cookie sheet without thawing and bake a few minutes longer than the specified time. If defrosted first, use the cooking time above. *Each pizza will make 6 servings.*

YEAST-RISING THICK
PIZZA CRUST

This is it, the yeast-rising thick pizza crust you've been hungering for. This is simple to make, freezes well, and will fool your friends into thinking they are eating pizza with a wheat crust.

2 cups rice flour
2 cups tapioca flour
²/₃ cup dry milk powder,
    or powdered baby
    formula, page x
3¹/₂ teaspoons xanthan
    gum
1 teaspoon salt
2 yeast cakes, or 2
    tablespoons dry yeast
    granules

1 cup lukewarm water,
    105° to 115°
1 tablespoon sugar
3 tablespoons shortening
¹/₂ cup hot water
4 egg whites, at room
    temperature

In bowl of your heavy-duty mixer, put flours, dried milk, xanthan gum, and salt. Crumble the yeast into the lukewarm water with the tablespoon of sugar added. Melt the shortening in the hot water.

With the mixer on low, blend the dry ingredients. Pour in the hot water and shortening, blending to mix. Add the egg whites, blend again, then add the yeast mixture. Beat on high speed for 4 minutes.

Spoon half the dough onto a greased cookie sheet or round pizza tin. With your hand in a plastic bag, pat the dough out in a circle about ¹/₄ inch thick except at the edges, which should be higher to contain the sauce and fillings. Repeat with the second half of the dough.

Spread immediately with your sauce and favorite toppings (see page 164). There is no need to let this rise, but by allowing 20 minutes of rise time, you will get an even thicker crust. Bake in preheated 400° oven for 20 to 22 minutes. *Makes two 12¹/₂-inch pizzas serving 8 to 12.*

PIZZA SAUCE AND TOPPINGS

There are gluten-free pizza sauces on the market, or you can make your own using this recipe from Jill Ryan.

One 8-ounce can tomato
sauce
1/2 teaspoon crushed
oregano leaves
Garlic powder

1/2 teaspoon dried crushed
basil
2 tablespoons sugar, or to
taste

Mix the above ingredients and spread them evenly over any 12-inch unbaked crust. Top with the following or anything you desire:

1 cup or more shredded mozzarella cheese
1 pound ground pork sausage, cooked in small chunks
and drained
One 2 1/4-ounce can sliced olives, drained
Sliced fresh mushrooms, if desired

Other toppings could include sardines, sliced salami, sliced green peppers, minced ham, a second cheese, or other items of your choice.

MINIPIZZA TRICKS

For a quick minipizza for a single serving try topping a thick corn tortilla with sauce and toppings. Bake in preheated 375° oven for approximately 12 minutes.

Another minipizza can be made for one person or enough for a crowd of hungry teenagers by slicing English Muffins (see page 104) and topping with sauce and cheese. Bake as above.

MAIN DISHES AND CASSEROLES

SEE ALSO
Cream of Chicken
   Soup (page 142)
Cream of Mushroom
   Soup (page 143)

SEE ALSO
Vegetable Quiche
   with Mashed Potato
   Crust (page 114)

Toad-in-the-Hole (page 115)
Overnight Casserole
   (page 116)
Pastas and Pasta Dishes
   (pages 150–159)

When I first started my gluten-free diet, I was content eating plain meats, potatoes, vegetables, and rice—and recovering my health. But it wasn't long before I found I craved the variety of flavors found only in mixed dishes, those bubbly with sauce, crunchy with varied textures, and rich with the odor of several foods combined.

In talking to other celiacs, I discovered that for most persons on a gluten-free diet, a steady diet of simply cooked meats and potatoes or rice becomes monotonous. Although we should remain suspicious and forgo that wonderful-smelling hot dish at a friend's table or at a restaurant, mixed dishes need not be forbidden at home.

In this section I include dishes that are favorites not only of mine but of my family and guests. As the cook, I don't like to prepare two separate meals; but I want others at the table to enjoy my GF food. Thus I've worked to make these mixed dishes both gluten free and tasty. So much so that I am often asked for the recipes by friends who can eat anything.

Many of these use rice, others potatoes, and some use nongluten bread. For the last, I use up my bread-making mistakes, or buy a gluten-free rice bread sold in some health food stores or ordered by mail (see the section on gluten-free products at the end of the book).

BROWN RICE PILAF

A popular, easy-to-make, nutty-tasting rice preparation to accompany barbecued ribs, baked chicken, or other dishes that don't have drippings from which make gravy. Serve it plain; the texture and flavor are so good it needs no sauce.

> 1 cup raw brown rice
> 2 1/2 cups beef stock, or water and GF powdered soup
>   base
> 2 teaspoons instant minced onion
> 1 teaspoon salt (if stock is unsalted)
> 1 tablespoon butter or margarine

Wash brown rice thoroughly and drain.

Bring stock, minced onions, and salt (if used) to boil. Add rice and butter. Bring back to a boil and stir.

Lower heat until water is just bubbling. Cover and simmer 45 to 50 minutes. Turn off heat. Remove lid and let stand 5 minutes to dry out.

To serve with chicken or turkey, I use chicken-flavored stock and add a stalk of celery thinly sliced. *Makes 3 cups cooked rice, about 6 servings.*

PILAF PLUS: For a tasty variation of the basic recipe, add to the rice when you stir it into the stock 1/2 to 1 cup sliced raw mushrooms, and 1/4 to 1/2 cup grated raw carrots.

SAUSAGE RICE CASSEROLE

A good way to use leftover pilaf, this moist meal-in-a-dish casserole is a favorite in our family. The recipe calls for pork sausage, but you can vary this by using ground beef or ground turkey. For a very easy meal, serve with tossed salad and fruit for dessert.

1 pound bulk pork sausage	1/2 cup diced celery
2 cups cooked brown rice	1 cup Basic White Sauce,
or Brown Rice Pilaf,	page 185 or Cream of
page 168	Chicken Soup, page 142
2 tablespoons diced onion	

In frying pan, brown the sausage. Drain off excess fat.

Place all ingredients in casserole and mix. Bake in preheated 325° oven for 50 to 60 minutes. *Makes 4 or 5 servings.*

BROCCOLI RICE SUPREME

This combination of vegetables, rice, and cheese is an all-round winner. For the cook it's easy to fix, can be done ahead, and freezes well, both before final cooking or as leftovers afterward. I think 1/2 to 1 cup diced ham is a nice addition to this dish, but it is delicious without it.

1 cup raw white rice	1/2 to 3/4 cup grated cheese
One 10-ounce box frozen	1 cup Mushroom Sauce,
chopped broccoli	page 186
1/2 cup minced onion	1 cup Cream of Chicken
1/2 cup thinly sliced celery	Soup, page 142
2 tablespoons butter or	
margarine	

Cook rice in 2 cups of water, following recipe on box or bag. Cook broccoli and drain thoroughly. Sauté onion and celery in butter until onion is clear.

Line large greased casserole or 9" × 13" glass baking dish with rice. Mix all the other ingredients together and pour over the rice. Refrigerate until ready to serve. This may be heated in the microwave approximately 6 to 8 minutes on high, until heated through, or baked in a preheated oven 45 minutes at 325°. *Makes 8 servings.*

If you add diced chicken or ham you will have a full meal in a dish.

CHINESE FRIED RICE

This is the Chinese trick for stretching a little leftover meat (pork, chicken, or beef) into a whole main dish, and is another tasty way of using leftover rice, either white or brown.

1/4 to 1/2 cup cooked meat	1/2 teaspoon salt
2 tablespoons oil	1 large egg
2 green onions, sliced thin	1 1/2 tablespoons soy sauce
2 cups cooked brown or white rice	Minced parsley for garnish, if desired

Cut meat in thin slivers.

Heat oil in large skillet, add green onions, and sauté about 2 minutes. Add meat and just heat through. Then add rice and salt and stir until all ingredients are blended. Beat egg with soy sauce and add to the rice, stirring rapidly so the mixture blends with the rice before setting. Cook until egg mixture is absorbed and the rice seems dry. This takes only a few minutes. Serve this oriental style by pressing rice into a bowl with a rounded bottom and then turning it out into a shallow dish, with the top now rounded. Garnish with minced parsley if you like. *Makes 4 servings.*

MY FAVORITE MEAT LOAF

This is a firm meat loaf that tastes delicious either hot or cold. It slices well when cold and makes great sandwiches.

1 pound extra-lean ground beef	1 tablespoon chili sauce
1 egg	1/3 cup GF cereal, crushed*
1 teaspoon instant minced onion	Salt and pepper to taste

Place all ingredients in mixing bowl and knead together with hands until well mixed. Form into rounded shape and place in a flat pan that has low raised sides to contain any drippings. Bake in preheated 350° oven 50 to 60 minutes. Let stand for 5 minutes before cutting in thin slices. *Makes 4 servings.*

*You may crush gluten-free rice or corn cereals, or save your bread mistakes or leftover bread and dry this in the oven. Then put in blender or food processor and grind into crumbs. (Be sure to dry bread first.)

MEATBALLS PIA

This recipe for meatballs baked in a tasty sauce came from an Italian friend in Alaska. The combination of the American cranberry with an Italian-flavored meat sauce is unusual but good.

Meatballs	Sauce
2 pounds ground meat	One 12-ounce bottle chili sauce
1 cup cornflakes	1 tablespoon lemon juice
1/3 cup chopped parsley	2 tablespoons brown sugar
2 eggs	One 16-ounce can cranberry jelly
2 tablespoons soy sauce	
1/4 teaspoon pepper	
1/3 cup catsup	
2 tablespoons dry minced onion	

In a bowl, mix together the meat, cornflakes, parsley, eggs, soy sauce, pepper, catsup, and dry onion. Form into 1-inch meatballs. Brown slightly in preheated 350° oven while you are mixing the sauce.

In a saucepan, place the chili sauce, lemon juice, brown sugar, and cranberry jelly. Heat until smooth and blended. Pour over the browned meatballs. Bake 30 to 35 minutes in 350° oven. *Makes 6 to 8 servings.*

MONTE CRISTO SANDWICH

A brunch or lunch favorite combining bread, meat, cheese, and eggs in one easy-to-serve hot sandwich. This recipe makes four sandwiches but could easily be cut to make a single portion.

8 slices GF bread	Butter or margarine to
2 tablespoons mayonnaise	spread
1 tablespoon mustard	2 eggs
4 thin slices cooked ham	1 tablespoon milk or
4 slices Swiss cheese	nondairy liquid
4 slices turkey or chicken	

Lay out the 8 slices of bread. In a small bowl, combine mayonnaise and mustard. Spread 4 slices of bread with the mixture. Top with 1 slice each of ham, cheese, and turkey. Spread butter on other 4 bread slices and complete the sandwiches.

Whisk together the eggs and milk. Dip the sandwiches (both sides) in the egg-milk mixture and cook on a preheated oiled griddle over medium (or slightly lower) heat until browned. Turn and brown other side. Try to cook each side about 5 minutes so the sandwiches will be heated through.

Serve to be eaten with knife and fork. This goes well with the Hot Curried Fruit on page 202 for brunch or with potato chips for a luncheon.

NO-FAIL CHEESE SOUFFLÉ

An easy soufflé that doesn't fall when you serve it. This is a fine luncheon dish, but with its rich cheese flavor, it is also a good meatless dinner. I like it with a topping of heated Mushroom Sauce (page 186).

1 1/2 cups milk or nondairy
   liquid
2 cups soft GF bread
   crumbs
1 1/2 cups grated Cheddar
   cheese

1 tablespoon butter
1/8 teaspoon paprika
1 teaspoon salt
3 eggs

In the top of a double boiler, place milk, bread crumbs, grated cheese, butter, and seasonings. Heat over hot water until the cheese is melted. Remove from heat and let cool slightly.

Meanwhile, separate the eggs. Beat the yolks slightly and add to the mixture in the double boiler. Beat whites until stiff. Fold them gently into the mixture. Pour into a greased 8″ × 8″ × 2″ baking dish set in a pan of hot water. Bake in a preheated 350° oven about 30 to 40 minutes, or until firm. Serve immediately. *Makes 6 servings.*

Any leftovers will keep in the refrigerator and can be reheated to serve at a later time.

CRUSTLESS SEAFOOD QUICHE

Who says real men don't eat quiche? This is a favorite with the men who've tasted it. There is no need for a crust because the rice flour forms a rich brown skin on the bottom of the quiche. For the cook's convenience, the batter may be made as far as a day ahead and refrigerated.

1/2 cup sliced mushrooms	1/4 cup sweet rice
2 tablespoons butter or	flour
margarine	1/4 teaspoon salt
4 eggs	2 cups grated Monterey
1 cup sour cream or	Jack cheese
nondairy substitute	6 ounces shrimp or
1 cup small-curd cottage	crab meat
cheese	

Sauté mushrooms in butter; then drain on paper towel.

In large mixing bowl, blend eggs, sour cream, cottage cheese, rice flour, and salt. Stir in mushrooms, grated cheese, and shrimp or crabmeat. Pour into a 9" or 10" quiche dish or deep pie plate sprayed with Pam or greased lightly.

Bake 45 minutes in preheated 350° oven, or until knife inserted near center comes out clean. Let stand 5 minutes before cutting. *Makes 6 servings.*

HAM AND CHEESE QUICHE: Substitute 1/2 to 3/4 cup diced ham for the crab or shrimp and use a small onion, diced, instead of the mushrooms.

TAMALE CASSEROLE

This corn dish makes a good change from potatoes and rice. When I first served this casserole to my husband, he asked why I always experimented on him. I replied that it was because he is a meat-and-potatoes man. When he went back for a second helping larger than the first, I knew this was a success.

1 small onion, chopped
1/2 medium green pepper, chopped
1 clove garlic, minced
1 tablespoon vegetable oil
3/4 pound lean ground beef
One 8-ounce can tomato sauce
One 8-ounce can whole-kernel corn

One 6 1/2-ounce can sliced black olives
1 cup milk or nondairy liquid
1/2 cup cornmeal
1/2 teaspoon salt
1 to 1 1/2 teaspoons chili powder
3/4 cup grated sharp Cheddar cheese

Sauté onion, pepper, and garlic in oil until onion is clear. Add beef and cook until browned. Pour off excess fat.

Add tomato sauce, drained corn, three-fourths of the olives, and the milk. Stir well, heat through, then add cornmeal, salt, and chili powder. Pour into well-greased 2-quart casserole. Decorate top with remaining olives.

Bake, covered, in preheated 350° oven for 45 minutes. Uncover and bake about 20 minutes more. For the last 5 minutes of baking, sprinkle cheese over the dish. It is ready when knife inserted in center comes out clean. *Makes 4 or 5 servings.* Recipe can easily be doubled.

MAYONNAISE CHICKEN CASSEROLE

A fine, moist casserole that can be made ahead and refrigerated before baking. This can be changed in many ways. Delete the mushrooms. Change the chicken to cooked ground turkey and add poultry seasoning to make it taste like turkey and dressing.

Butter or margarine
6 slices GF bread
2 cups cooked chicken
1/4 cup diced onion
1/2 cup sliced celery
One 6 1/2-ounce can sliced mushrooms, or 1/3 pound fresh mushrooms, sliced

3/4 teaspoon salt
Dash of pepper
2 tablespoons sweet rice flour
2 eggs
1/2 cup mayonnaise
2 1/2 cups milk or nondairy liquid

Butter bread and cut into cubes. Toss chicken, onion, celery, drained mushrooms, seasonings, and sweet rice flour together.

In a buttered 2-quart casserole, layer a third of the bread with half the chicken mixture. Add a third more bread and rest of mixture. Top with bread.

Beat the eggs slightly. Blend in mayonnaise and milk until smooth. Pour this over bread and chicken.

Bake in preheated 325° oven for 1 hour, until set. *Makes 4 servings.*

BETTE'S BEST CHICKEN POTPIE

After watching my husband order chicken potpie at restaurants, I realized I was denying him, as well as myself, this old favorite. When I tried one at home, it was so successful that he now compares all others to mine. This recipe makes a large amount, but, as with many other casserole dishes, the flavor is even better the second day. The secret is the topping of tender buttermilk biscuits. With a tossed salad, this makes a complete meal.

1 cup cooked chicken	2 to 3 tablespoons water
2 cups chicken stock	1/4 cup cream or nondairy
1/2 cup diced carrots	substitute
1/2 cup sliced celery	Salt and pepper to taste
1/4 cup minced onion	1 recipe Buttermilk Biscuit
1/2 cup frozen peas	dough, page 43, sugar
3 tablespoons rice flour	omitted

Dice the chicken and set aside. Place chicken stock in large saucepan and bring to a boil. Add carrots, celery, and onions and cook for 15 minutes. Then add peas and chicken and cook 5 minutes longer.

Mix the rice flour to a thin paste with a few tablespoons of water. Thicken the stock with the rice flour paste and cook on low for a minute or two. Add cream or nondairy liquid and season with salt and pepper. (If the stock is salted, you probably won't need any more.)

Pour the cooked potpie mixture into a 2-quart casserole and top with 2 1/2-inch rounds of biscuit dough. Bake all together in a preheated 350° oven for about 20 to 25 minutes. *Makes 5 or 6 servings.*

This recipe can be made ahead and refrigerated to be baked just before serving. The biscuits still rise but might take a bit longer to bake. Watch the oven and check the cooking. When the filling is bubbly and the biscuits a warm brown, the dish is ready to serve.

SCALLOPED POTATOES
AND HAM

This is a time-saver for the gluten-free cook, for it makes its own sauce.

> 4 large potatoes, peeled and sliced thin
> 1 cup cooked ham, cut into slivers
> Salt and pepper to taste (onion salt gives extra flavor)
> 2 cups milk or nondairy liquid
> 3 tablespoons sweet rice or white rice flour
> 1/2 cup mayonnaise

Layer potatoes and ham in 1 1/2-quart casserole, adding salt and pepper to the layers.

In a bowl, mix a few tablespoons of the milk with rice flour and mayonnaise. Blend with whisk until smooth. Then add remaining milk. Blend again until smooth. Pour over the potatoes.

Bake in preheated 350° oven for 1 hour, or until potatoes test done and the sauce is bubbly and thick. *Makes 5 or 6 servings.*

POTATOES AU GRATIN: For cheese lovers, use the recipe above but omit the ham and use 3/4 cup grated Cheddar cheese layered with the potatoes. Or use the Cheese Sauce recipe on page 186, thinned with milk, instead of the milk, flour, and mayonnaise mixture.

GONE-FOR-THE-DAY STEW

This easy but delicious stew was created by one of my skiing friends who didn't want to steal from her time on the slopes to cook. She stuck the casserole in the oven after breakfast and we'd return tired and hungry at the end of the day to a full main dish ready and waiting.

1 to 1 1/2 pounds beef stew
   meat
One 24-ounce package
   frozen stew vegetables*
1 cup Cream of Celery
   Sauce, page 187

One 13-ounce can onion
   soup
One 14 1/2-ounce can beef
   broth

Brown the meat. Place in a 4-quart casserole or dutch oven, then toss in all the other ingredients. Cover. Put dish in oven set at 225° and forget it for 6 to 8 hours. Serve. There is no extra work here, for the combination of soups makes a zesty, creamy gravy seasoned to perfection. This also makes a good overnight Crockpot dish. *Makes 6 to 8 servings.*

*Or use 1/2 cup small pearl onions, 1 cup celery cut in 1/3-inch slices, 1 1/2 cups carrots sliced in 1/2-inch slices, and 1 1/2 cups small round potatoes or larger potatoes cut into 1- to 1 1/2-inch chunks.

SAUSAGE AND LENTIL BAKE

The high protein in lentils plus the spicy sausage make this a winner for taste and nutrition. This makes a large dish and is even better the next day, or frozen and heated again for another meal.

1 cup dried lentils	1 cup sliced celery
2 cups water	1 cup chopped onions
2 teaspoons instant beef broth granules	1 teaspoon dried minced garlic
8 ounces kielbasa sausage	1/4 cup catsup
One 16-ounce can tomatoes	1 teaspoon prepared mustard
	3 tablespoons brown sugar

Wash lentils and pick over carefully. Drain. Put water and broth granules in 4-quart dutch oven and bring to boil over high heat. Meanwhile, cut sausage into 1/4-inch-thick rounds. Purée the tomatoes. Prepare other vegetables.

Add all the ingredients to the stock and let contents come back to boil. Boil briskly for about 30 seconds, stirring constantly.

Reduce heat to low. Cover the pot, leaving lid slightly ajar. Simmer 45 to 50 minutes, until lentils are tender. If mixture seems too thick, stir in 1/4 cup water. Serve with a tossed salad for a full meal. *Makes 6 to 8 servings.*

EASY ENCHILADAS

Don't pass this one up! I served it to unexpected company and they raved. It takes only a few minutes to prepare and about 15 minutes to cook.

1 pound ground beef	1 1/2 cups water
One 8-ounce can tomato sauce	8 thick corn tortillas
1 package enchilada sauce mix	1/2 cup grated Cheddar cheese

In a frying pan, brown the ground beef. Meanwhile, combine tomato sauce, enchilada sauce mix, and water in saucepan. Bring to a boil; simmer 5 minutes.

Drain fat off the ground beef and stir $1/2$ cup of sauce into meat.

Dip each tortilla into sauce. Put 3 tablespoons meat filling on each. Roll tortillas around filling and place, seam sides down, in 8" × 12" × 2" baking dish.

Spread remaining sauce evenly over enchiladas and top with grated cheese. Bake in preheated 350° oven for 15 minutes, or slightly longer if desired. *Makes 4 servings.*

CROWD PLEASERS

For celiacs, going past the hot dishes at a picnic or potluck supper is as frustrating as walking past a bakery. We have to avoid every mixed dish, for many obviously contain pasta. Other dishes are suspect, for they might contain gluten in the form of canned creamed soups or wheat flour thickening.

To avoid this disappointment, take your own main dish. The following have proved popular with my guests, and are safely gluten free.

HOMEMADE CHILI

Chili is a simple crowd pleaser, especially a young crowd. It's easy to make, inexpensive, and gluten free.

2 pounds ground beef
1 large onion, chopped,
plus 3 tablespoons finely
chopped onion, for
garnish
Two 28-ounce cans stewed
tomatoes
Two 15-ounce cans chili
beans
One 15-ounce can kidney
beans

One or two 6-ounce cans
Spicy Hot V8 vegetable
juice
2 tablespoons sugar
2 tablespoons chili powder
$1/2$ teaspoon garlic powder
$3/4$ teaspoon onion powder
$1/2$ cup grated Cheddar
cheese, for garnish

Brown meat in a large kettle. Add chopped onion and cook until onion is clear. Then add remaining ingredients except garnishes, using the bean liquid and as much of the Spicy Hot V8 as you need to achieve the desired consistency. Simmer on back of stove for at least 1 hour, preferably longer. *Makes 18 to 20 servings.*

This may be made a day ahead and reheated, or may simmer for hours on the stove until ready to serve.

For an added touch, serve topped with grated Cheddar cheese and finely chopped raw onion.

CALICO BEANS

This mixture of several kinds of beans with the ground beef gives it a different flavor from the usual baked bean hot dishes at potlucks and picnics. This recipe makes a lot, and can be mixed up ahead of time and baked at the last hour. Any leftovers can be frozen, but because this is a favorite with men and boys, there are seldom any leftovers.

4 or 5 strips bacon	1/2 cup catsup
1 pound extra-lean ground beef	1 teaspoon salt
One 28-ounce can GF pork and beans	3/4 cup brown sugar
One 15-ounce can kidney beans	1 teaspoon prepared mustard
One 17-ounce can small lima beans	2 tablespoons wine vinegar

Cut bacon into small bits. Brown it in a skillet with beef. Drain off any extra fat. Put in large casserole and add beans, drained slightly.

Mix catsup, salt, brown sugar, mustard, and vinegar and stir into the beans and meat mixture. This can now be refrigerated until 40 minutes before serving time or baked and reheated for serving.

Bake 40 minutes in preheated 350° oven. *Makes 18 to 20 servings.*

HAWAIIAN CURRY

Before I was served this marvelous mild, sweet curry in Hawaii, I was sure I could never learn to enjoy this unusual dish. But it is not at all like the strong Indian curries. I have served it often to others who aren't fond of curry and have always had compliments.

It takes more time to prepare than the other dishes for a crowd, so save this for your favorite guests. They will love you for it.

One 5- to 6-pound chicken
1 medium onion
2 cloves garlic
3 inches fresh gingerroot
3/4 cup (1 1/2 sticks) butter
  or margarine
3/4 cup sweet rice flour

1/4 cup curry powder*
1/4 cup sugar
Salt to taste
2 cups milk or nondairy
  liquid
One 7 3/4-ounce can
  coconut milk†

Boil chicken in water to cover; let cool in the broth. Remove meat and cut into cubes. Save 2 cups of the broth for the curry.

Chop the onion, mince the garlic, and grate the gingerroot. Sauté these in the butter in a large pan. Add the flour, curry, salt, and sugar. Do not allow mixture to burn or lump. Slowly add the reserved 2 cups chicken broth and cook until well blended and smooth. Boil a little, stirring constantly.

Add milk and coconut milk; do not let boil. Add the cubed chicken and put pan over hot water. Keep water at a simmer and cook the curry for 4 hours, stirring often. You may need to add more chicken broth if sauce gets too thick, or more sugar or salt to taste. *Makes 12 to 16 servings.*

Serve your curry with cooked white rice and an assortment of the traditional condiments: mango chutney, bacon bits, chopped macadamia nuts, chopped green onion tops, fresh shredded coconut. Some people use chopped hard-boiled eggs, but I prefer to stuff the eggs and serve separately. I also like to serve Baked Bananas, page 201, as a side dish for this company spread.

This should serve 16, but most people come back for seconds and thirds, so plan on that. I double the recipe, going a bit easy on the flour. The amount of chicken can vary. It doesn't have to be doubled.

This is a good way to use your Thanksgiving or Christmas turkey leftovers to serve a crowd.

---

*Curry powder is a mixed spice, so check the ingredients list on the label. As of this book's publication date, Crescent is known to be gluten free. (Others may be, but check before using.)
†If you can't find coconut milk, use shredded, unsweetened coconut to taste (about 1/4 cup) and increase amount of milk by 1 cup.

SAUCES FOR CASSEROLES

For the gluten-free cook there is no reaching for a can of cream soup to make an easy sauce. Most prepared soups contain some wheat flour and have to be avoided. Here are a few quick sauces that can substitute for a can of soup in recipes in your other cookbooks. Freeze in 1-cup amounts.

See also Cream of Chicken Soup (page 142) and Cream of Mushroom Soup (page 143). There are also a few dehydrated soups, such as Hain and Med Diet, that are gluten free.

BASIC WHITE SAUCE

The sweet rice flour used in this and many of the other recipes is a superior thickening agent, for it inhibits liquid separation if the food is to be frozen.

4 tablespoons (1/2 stick)
   butter or margarine
1 3/4 cups milk
1/4 teaspoon salt
1/8 teaspoon pepper

2 1/2 tablespoons sweet rice
   flour
Optional: 1 tablespoon
   chopped green onion
   tops

Melt butter in saucepan over low heat. Add 1 1/2 cups of the milk, salt, and pepper. Bring the mixture to warm but do not boil.

In a small bowl, make a paste of the rice flour and the remaining 1/4 cup milk. Add slowly to the heating mixture. Continue cooking over low heat until thickened, stirring constantly to prevent burning.

This is especially good for casseroles with 1 tablespoon chopped green onion tops added. *Makes about 1 pint sauce.*

CHEESE SAUCE

This sauce goes well with casseroles using potatoes, rice, or pasta.

2 tablespoons chopped
onion
1 tablespoon butter or
margarine
1 tablespoon sweet rice
flour
3/4 cup chicken stock

2 cups milk or nondairy
liquid
3/4 cup grated Cheddar
cheese
Salt and paprika for
seasoning

In a saucepan, sauté the onion in the butter until clear. Then stir in the rice flour. Blend well.

Add the stock slowly, stirring as you pour it in. When the sauce is smooth and boiling, add the milk. Heat the soup but don't let it boil, and then add the grated cheese.

Season to taste with salt and paprika. Remember that if the stock is salted, you will probably need little additional salt. *Makes 3 cups sauce.*

MUSHROOM SAUCE

Here is a tasty, easy-to-make sauce for casseroles.

One 4-ounce can
mushrooms, drained, or
1/2 cup sliced fresh
mushrooms
1 1/2 teaspoons dry minced
onion

2 tablespoons rice flour
One 14-ounce can chicken
stock
1/2 cup rich cream or
nondairy liquid
Salt and pepper to taste

Place the mushrooms, minced onion, and rice flour in blender. Add 1/2 cup of the chicken stock. Blend slightly. Add the rest of the stock and blend again. The mushrooms can remain in small chunks or be minced.

Place the blended mix in a saucepan and cook until thickened. Then add the cream and cook a minute or two, stirring constantly. The sauce will be quite thick. At this point, season to taste. If the stock was salted, it will need very little more seasoning.

For use, thin to desired consistency with milk or nondairy liquid or with water for the casserole of your choice. *Makes about 3 cups thick sauce.*

CREAM OF CELERY SAUCE

This is fine as a soup, but I like it best as the binding liquid in casseroles. Freeze any left over.

1 cup or more chopped celery	2 cups milk or nondairy liquid
1/3 cup minced onion	1 1/2 tablespoons sweet rice flour
1 tablespoon butter	
2 cups chicken stock	

Chop celery, including tops if you wish. Sauté celery and onion in butter until onion is clear, about 2 minutes.

Add the stock, bring to boil, turn down heat, and simmer for 3 minutes. Strain the soup or cool slightly and put in blender or food processor and blend until vegetables are puréed.

Return to saucepan and add 1 1/2 cups of the milk. To the rest of the milk add the rice flour and then stir this paste into the hot sauce. Bring to the boiling point and cook for 1 minute. *Makes about 4 cups sauce.*

FRUIT FANCIES

Plain fruits, either fresh or canned, are among the few desserts one can safely order out on a gluten-free diet. We pick them from the buffet trays and notice them on any menu. But fruits in any baked form in a restaurant or at a friend's house have to be suspect.

Here I've put together a small collection of ways of using fresh, canned, or frozen fruit in baking for brunch, lunch, or dinner. Some of them are old familiars with a change to our gluten-free flours. Others may be new to you. All are enthusiastically endorsed by friends who don't have to stick to any diet.

For some of the baking in this section I suggest using my gluten-free flour mix. For your convenience I'll repeat the formula:

2 parts white rice flour
2/3 part potato starch flour
1/3 part tapioca flour

FRUIT-FILLED MERINGUES

When a friend called desperately about a dinner party she was hosting and asked, "Have you any suggestions for dessert you can eat? I don't have any of your flour to bake with," I replied, "Why not meringues? They don't take flour."

It's a good answer, but don't leave them for someone else to try.

Meringues are very simple to make and can be made several days ahead and stored in a closed container. All you need are:

> 3 egg whites
> 1/4 teaspoon cream of tartar
> 3/4 cup sugar
> Fresh or frozen berries for filling

In a metal or glass bowl, beat egg whites and cream of tartar until frothy. Gradually beat in the sugar, a little at a time, until mixture is very stiff and glossy.

Drop by spoonfuls in 3 1/2-inch circles 1 1/2 inches thick on brown paper on a baking sheet. With the back of a spoon make an indentation on each meringue. Bake in preheated 275° oven for about 1 hour. Turn oven off and leave the meringues in until oven has cooled.

To serve, fill with fresh or frozen and thawed berries and, if desired, top with whipped cream. *Makes 6 meringues.*

HAWAIIAN DELIGHT MERINGUES

A fancy-looking dessert that takes but minutes of the cook's time.

> One 30-ounce can
>   pineapple slices
> 2 bananas
> 1 tablespoon lemon juice
> 3 tablespoons plus 1/2 cup
>   sugar
>
> 1/2 teaspoon cinnamon
> 4 egg whites
> 1/4 teaspoon cream of
>   tartar

Drain the pineapple slices and arrange in a large buttered baking dish or on a buttered cookie sheet. Cut each banana into 5 pieces and place one piece on each slice of pineapple. Sprinkle with lemon juice.

Mix the 3 tablespoons of sugar with the cinnamon and sprinkle half of this over the fruits.

Beat the egg whites with the cream of tartar until soft peaks form. Add the rest of the sugar (reserving 1 tablespoon) a couple of tablespoons at a time, beating well after each addition. Beat until the whites form stiff peaks.

Spread the meringue over pineapple and bananas, using a swirling design. Sprinkle the remaining sugar over the meringues and bake in a preheated 400° oven for 10 minutes, or until meringue is brown. Serve warm or cold.

If you are using fresh pineapple, peel, core, and cut into 10 slices. The pineapple does not need to be precooked. *Makes 8 to 10 servings.*

PEACH CUSTARD PIE

An easy to make custard and fruit pie in a crisp, buttery crust. A summertime favorite when peaches are ripe. Also great with an apple filling rather than the peach.

1 1/2 cups GF cereal	1/2 teaspoon cinnamon
2 tablespoons sugar	1/2 cup brown sugar,
3 tablespoons butter or	packed
margarine	2 eggs
3 medium-sized peaches	1 cup sour cream or
1 tablespoon lemon juice	nondairy substitute

Crush the cereal in a plastic bag and add the sugar. Melt the butter, pour into bag, and mix. Pat into deep 9″ pie plate.

Slice the peaches into a bowl. Add lemon juice, cinnamon, and brown sugar, reserving 1 tablespoonful of sugar. Toss lightly and place on the cereal crust. Bake in preheated 375° oven for 15 minutes.

While this is baking, beat the eggs and add the sour cream and the remaining tablespoon of brown sugar. Pour this over the partly baked peaches and return to the oven for 20 to 25 minutes, until the custard jiggles very slightly.

Serve warm or cool. Will keep, covered with plastic wrap, in refrigerator for up to 2 days. *Makes 6 to 8 servings.*

For apple filling, put apple, lemon juice, spice, and sugar mixture in microwave for 3 minutes before pouring into cereal crust and baking. In the oven it takes a bit longer to bake before pouring on the custard topping.

DEEP-DISH BERRY PIE WITH A CREAM CHEESE CRUST

A real crowd pleaser that is also good with other juicy fruits like peaches and plums. The recipe is given for an 8" × 8" baking dish but can be doubled for a 9" × 13" pan.

Filling	Crust
5 1/2 cups berries (blueberries, blackberries, raspberries, boysenberries, loganberries, or other)	One 3-ounce package cream cheese
	2 tablespoons butter or margarine
1 cup sugar, or to taste	2 teaspoons sugar
3 tablespoons tapioca flour	3/4 cup GF flour mix

Wash and drain berries. Pour about a fourth of them into an 8" × 8" pan and mash. Toss the remaining whole berries with sugar and flour and add. Put aside while making the crust.

Put cream cheese, butter, and sugar into a mixing bowl and beat with an electric mixer until well blended. Add the flour and mix again until blended. Roll dough into ball and refrigerate until firm enough to roll easily, about 30 minutes.

Place the chilled pastry on plastic wrap, cover with another piece of plastic wrap, and roll until slightly larger than the pan. Remove top plastic and turn the pastry over onto the berries before removing the other plastic. (This makes for easy handling.) Tuck the crust overlap down the sides of the pan into your berries. Bake in preheated 350° oven for approximately 1 to 1 1/4 hours. *Makes 6 servings.*

PEAR TORTE

This is another fruit and custard baked in a crust, but a bit more elegant than the peach custard pie. Pears are often overlooked in baking by cooks more familiar with apples or berries, but this treat will show they shouldn't be.

Crust

1/2 cup (1 stick) butter or margarine
1/3 cup sugar
1/2 teaspoon vanilla
1/2 cup rice flour
1/4 cup cornstarch
1/4 cup tapioca flour
1/2 teaspoon salt

Filling

1/2 cup sour cream or nondairy substitute
One 3-ounce package cream cheese
1/4 cup sugar
1 egg
1/2 teaspoon vanilla

Topping

2 cups peeled, sliced pears
1 tablespoon lemon juice
3 tablespoons brown sugar
1 teaspoon cinnamon
1/3 cup apricot preserves

For the crust, cream together the butter and sugar, then beat in the vanilla. Add the flours and salt. Blend and press into a greased, deep 9″ pie tin or springform pan. Bake for 10 minutes in preheated 375° oven. Leave oven on.

Meanwhile, prepare the filling: Beat the sour cream and cream cheese together. Add the sugar, egg, and vanilla, beating until smooth. Pour this over the partially baked crust.

Top with the sliced pears, which have been gently tossed with the lemon juice, brown sugar, and cinnamon. For a more elegant look, arrange the slices in two overlapping circles. Warm the apricot preserves and brush over the pears. Bake at 375° for 45 to 55 minutes, or until golden brown. Cool slightly before serving. (It is also good cold.) *Makes 6 to 8 servings.*

BERRY COBBLER

This quick-and-easy baked dessert can be made of either fresh or frozen blackberries, loganberries, or blueberries.

1 quart berries	1/4 teaspoon salt
2 cups sugar	1/2 cup milk or nondairy
2 tablespoons shortening	liquid
2 eggs	1/4 teaspoon vanilla
1 cup GF flour mix	Whipped cream for garnish
2 teaspoons baking powder	

Put berries and 1 1/2 cups sugar in a metal or flameproof 8″ × 10″ baking pan. Over them pour enough water to barely cover the berries. Place the pan on stove and slowly bring to boiling point. Meanwhile, mix up the batter.

In a mixing bowl, cream together the remaining 1/2 cup sugar and the shortening. Beat in the eggs. Sift together the flour, baking powder, and salt; add alternately with the milk. Don't overbeat. Stir in the vanilla.

Drop this by tablespoonfuls over the boiling fruit. Bake in preheated 350° oven for about 25 to 30 minutes. The topping will spread out over the fruit. Serve hot, dishing up topping and fruit together. Garnish with whipped cream. *Makes 8 to 10 servings.*

APPLE CHEESE CRISP

A gluten-free twist to the old crisp that called for oatmeal. Try this on your family. Mine loved it.

Filling

6 cups peeled, sliced apples
  (4 to 5 apples)
1 1/4 teaspoons cinnamon
1/4 teaspoon nutmeg
Dash of salt
1 cup sugar
1 tablespoon lemon juice

Topping

1 cup GF flour mix
1/2 cup brown sugar
6 tablespoons (3/4 stick)
  butter or margarine
1 cup grated Cheddar
  cheese

Peel and slice the apples into a large mixing bowl. Tumble with the spices, salt, sugar, and lemon juice. Pour out into a 9″ × 13″ baking pan. In a smaller bowl, place the flour and brown sugar. Cut in the butter until the mixture feels like cornmeal. Then mix in the grated cheese. Crumble this topping over the apples. Bake uncovered in a preheated 350° oven for 1 hour. May be served hot or cold. *Makes 10 to 12 servings.*

RHUBARB CRUMBLE

Another twist on the old crisp. Rhubarb lovers beware: This is addictive. Top with yogurt or sour cream for an extra special dessert.

Filling

1¼ cups sugar
1 tablespoon tapioca
 flour
½ teaspoon cinnamon
4 cups sliced fresh rhubarb
 or one 16-ounce package
 frozen

Topping

¾ cup GF flour mix
½ cup brown sugar
⅛ teaspoon salt
½ cup (1 stick) butter or
 margarine
½ cup GF bread crumbs
 or Perky's Nutty Rice
 cereal

In a small dish, combine sugar, flour, and cinnamon. Mix this with the rhubarb and place in a shallow 9″ × 9″ baking pan. For the topping, combine flour, sugar, and salt. Cut in the butter or margarine. Stir in the bread crumbs or cereal. Sprinkle this mixture over the rhubarb. Bake 1 hour in preheated 350° oven. Serve warm. *Makes 8 servings.*

LIME SPONGE PUDDING

The lime gives a new taste to the old lemon sponge. It is cake and pudding made together.

3 eggs
1½ cups milk
2 tablespoons butter or
 margarine
1 cup sugar

½ cup GF flour mix
⅓ cup lime juice
1 tablespoon grated lime
 peel

Separate the eggs. Place the yolks in a medium-sized bowl, the whites in another bowl to whip later.

Scald the milk. Then beat the egg yolks and slowly whisk or blend in the milk. Melt the butter and add with the sugar, flour, lime juice, and peel.

Beat the egg whites until stiff and fold them into the lime mixture. Spoon into 8 custard cups and arrange the cups in a 9″ × 13″ baking pan. Add hot water to 1 inch around the cups. Bake 22 to 25 minutes in preheated 325° oven. Serve at room temperature or chilled. *Makes 8 servings.*

BLACKBERRY DUMPLINGS

On our family camping trips, my mother, with four children begging for dessert and no oven, created this top-of-the-stove or over-the-campfire treat. It may be made with huckleberries (the original), blueberries, loganberries, or any other juicy fruit you wish.

Sauce

1 quart fresh or frozen
   berries
1 cup water (to barely
   cover fruit)
1 1/2 cups sugar, or to taste
1 tablespoon lemon juice

Dumplings

2 tablespoons sugar

3 tablespoons shortening
1 egg
1/3 cup buttermilk or sour
   milk
1/2 cup rice flour
1/3 cup potato starch flour
2 teaspoons baking powder
1/2 teaspoon baking soda
1/2 teaspoon salt

Place the berries, water, sugar, and lemon juice in a 4-quart saucepan on the stove. Bring to a gentle boil while making the dumplings.

In mixing bowl, cream the sugar and shortening. Beat in the egg. Stir in the buttermilk alternately with the sifted dry ingredients. Do not overbeat. This will be a fairly stiff dough.

Drop dough by 8 small spoonfuls onto the boiling fruit sauce. Cover, turn to simmer, and cook without peeking for 20 minutes.

Serve hot in small bowls with the fruit sauce spooned over the dumpling. Top with cream, whipped cream, or ice cream. *Makes 8 servings.*

FRUIT CRÊPES
WITH WINE SAUCE

Wine sauce can be used with many fruits in many ways. Serve the sauce and fruit over sponge cake, waffles, GF ice cream, or yogurt. The fruit can be a mixture of apples, peaches, bananas, or others.

1 recipe Crêpes, page 108
1¹/₂ to 2 cups cut-up fruit
Lemon juice
4 tablespoons (¹/₂ stick) butter or margarine
¹/₂ cup dark brown sugar
¹/₂ teaspoon cinnamon
¹/₄ teaspoon nutmeg
¹/₃ cup dry white wine

Make the crêpes and prepare the fruit; squeeze lemon juice over the fruit to keep it from discoloring.

Combine butter, brown sugar, spices, and wine in a small saucepan. Bring to a boil, then turn to simmer, stirring constantly for 10 minutes or until slightly thickened into a syrup.

Roll a small amount of fruit in each crêpe, place crêpes seam side down in a lightly buttered 9″ × 9″ baking dish, and top with the syrup. Bake in a preheated 325° oven for about 15 minutes, or microwave for a few minutes. Serve warm. *Makes 4 to 6 servings.*

BAKED APPLES WITH NUTS
AND RAISINS

A simple winter dessert spiced up for company.

4 large baking apples	1 tablespoon brown sugar
2 tablespoons raisins	1 tablespoon butter or
2 tablespoons chopped	margarine
walnuts	1/2 cup water
1 teaspoon cinnamon	

Peel skin from the top of the apples to about 1 inch down. Core the apples, trying not to cut all the way through to the bottom. Arrange in an 8″ × 8″ baking dish.

In a small bowl, combine the raisins, walnuts, cinnamon, and brown sugar. Stuff each apple center with equal amounts of the mixture. Dot the tops with butter. Pour the water around the apples and bake in preheated 375° oven for 45 minutes, or until tender but not mushy, basting occasionally with the juicy water.

Serve warm or cool topped with whipped cream or yogurt. *Makes 4 servings.*

BAKED BANANAS

A fine accompaniment to pork, ham, teriyaki chicken, or curry, or serve them as a dessert. These are simple to prepare and can be made earlier in the day to pop into the oven just before dinner is served. Or bake earlier and serve at room temperature.

4 firm eating bananas or	1 cup crushed cornflakes
special baking bananas	3 tablespoons honey
such as plantains	3 tablespoons lemon juice

Grease an 8″ × 8″ baking dish generously with butter. Peel bananas and cut in half. Roll each section in the crushed cornflakes, pressing slightly so the banana is thoroughly coated. Arrange banana sections in the baking dish. Stir the honey and lemon juice together and drizzle all the sections with the mixture, making sure the bananas are coated.

Bake in preheated 350° oven for 20 minutes. Serve hot or at room temperature. *Makes 4 servings.*

HOT CURRIED FRUIT

This spicy mixed fruit casserole from Jan Winkelman is a fine accompaniment for chicken and rice. Or try it at a brunch to complement ham and sweet rolls.

One 16-ounce can peach halves	¹/₄ cup (¹/₂ stick) margarine
One 16-ounce can pear halves	¹/₂ cup brown sugar
One 13¹/₂-ounce can sliced pineapple or pineapple chunks	1 teaspoon curry powder
	Maraschino cherries, for garnish

Drain the fruits, saving the juice. Arrange the fruit attractively in a shallow casserole dish.

In a saucepan, mix together ¹/₄ cup of the reserved fruit juice, the margarine, brown sugar, and curry powder. Heat until the margarine melts. Pour over the fruit and bake in preheated 350° oven for about 30 minutes. Garnish with the cherries before serving hot. *Makes 6 to 8 servings.*

If a larger casserole of fruit is desired, add one 17-ounce can of apricot halves to the above recipe and increase the curry to 1¹/₄ teaspoons powder, or to taste. *Makes 8 to 10 servings.*

WINE CURRIED FRUIT

This is a much larger and more elegant casserole of curried fruit to serve at a dinner or buffet.

2 bananas
One 29-ounce can peach
  halves
One 26-ounce can pear
  halves
One 20-ounce can
  pineapple chunks
Two 6¹/₂-ounce cans
  mandarin oranges

One 8-ounce jar
  maraschino cherries
¹/₂ cup (1 stick) butter
¹/₂ cup brown sugar
1 tablespoon cornstarch
¹/₂ cup dry white wine
1 teaspoon curry
  powder

Slice the bananas diagonally in 1¹/₂-inch chunks. Drain all the other fruit and arrange all in a 2¹/₂-quart baking dish. Combine the butter, sugar, cornstarch, wine, and curry powder in a saucepan and cook, stirring constantly, until slightly thickened. Pour over the fruit. Bake, uncovered, in preheated 350° oven for about 15 to 20 minutes. Serve hot. *Makes 12 to 14 servings.*

HOLIDAY FARE

BREADS AND STUFFINGS

DESSERTS

SEE ALSO

For most of us, holidays have always been associated with special foods—cherry pie on Washington's birthday, hot cross buns at Easter, and turkey and dressing at Thanksgiving. There is no reason to forgo any of these dishes because we have to maintain a gluten-free diet.

Many of the old favorites convert easily to our flours with tasty results. And for other things, like dressing for that Thanksgiving turkey, I have several suggestions.

All of these recipes have been tested on family and friends, and most agreed they were as good as, if not better than, their old holiday favorites.

BREADS AND STUFFINGS

LATKES (Potato Pancakes)

Potato pancakes have always been a Hanukkah tradition. Little girls learned how to grate the potatoes and test the texture at their mother's side in the Jewish kitchen. It was hard work, but with the food processor, most of the work is taken out of this dish. It's too good to save just for the holiday.

3 fist-sized potatoes
1 onion about 2 1/2 inches
  round
2 eggs

2 tablespoons rice flour
1/2 teaspoon salt
1/4 teaspoon pepper

Peel and quarter the potatoes and place in a bowl of water until ready to process. In the blender, pulse the onion until finely chopped. Remove to mixing bowl and then pulse the potatoes in several batches until chopped fine. Beat the eggs. Add them with the flour and seasonings to the potatoes and onions. Mix well.

Fry the pancakes in about 1/4 inch of hot oil until golden, about 3 to 4 minutes per side. Serve hot. *Makes 9 to 10 pancakes.*

Traditionally latkes are fried in hot oil, but if you don't mind defying tradition, they turn out delicious cooked on a very lightly greased Teflon pan.

HOT CROSS BUNS

Now you can have them, too, those cinnamony buns with the icing cross that appear in the bake shops only at Easter.

2 cups white rice flour
2/3 cup tapioca flour
1/3 cup potato starch flour
1/3 cup plus 2 teaspoons
  sugar
2/3 cup dry powdered
  milk or baby formula
  (see page x)
3 1/2 teaspoons xanthan
  gum
1 1/2 teaspoons salt
2 teaspoons cinnamon

1 1/2 yeast cakes or 1 1/2
  tablespoons dry yeast
  granules
1 1/2 cups water
1/4 cup shortening
3 eggs
1 teaspoon vinegar
1 cup white raisins
1 egg yolk for brushing
2 tablespoons water for
  brushing

Combine flours, 1/3 cup sugar, powdered milk, xanthan gum, salt, and cinnamon in bowl of mixer. Break or sprinkle the yeast into 1/2 cup lukewarm water with 2 teaspoons sugar added and let dissolve. Melt the shortening in 1 cup of water in a saucepan.

Pour shortening water into dry ingredients. Blend with mixer. Add eggs and beat for a few seconds. The mixture should be slightly warm. Then add the dissolved yeast and the vinegar. Beat with mixer at highest speed for 2 minutes. Stir in raisins.

Place the mixing bowl, tightly covered with plastic wrap, in a warm place and let rise until doubled, approximately 1 to 1 1/2 hours.

Return dough to mixer and beat for 3 minutes. Prepare two 8″ × 8″ pans or 18 muffin cups by greasing and lightly flouring with rice flour. With greased hands pinch up dough enough to make a bun about 2 1/2 inches around and 1 1/2 inches high. Dough will be sticky, but form it into rolls, 9 to a pan. When rolls are formed, brush them (fingers work fine) with a mixture of the egg yolk and the water. Let the buns rise again about 1 hour.

Bake in preheated 375° oven for approximately 35 minutes. While still slightly warm, ice a cross on top with a frosting blended of:

> 1/4 cup powdered sugar
> 1 teaspoon butter
> Cream to moisten to desired consistency

Makes 18 rolls or muffin-size buns.

CHRISTMAS STOLLEN

An excellent Christmas bread. This one uses no yeast, but the ricotta cheese makes it a taste winner.

3 cups GF flour mix	3 tablespoons candied fruit
1 tablespoon plus 2 teaspoons baking powder	2 tablespoons light raisins
	1 tablespoon sliced almonds
1/4 teaspoon salt	1 tablespoon grated lemon peel
3 teaspoons xanthan gum	
2 cups ricotta cheese	1 tablespoon melted butter
4 large eggs, beaten	1 tablespoon powdered sugar
2/3 cup sugar	

Combine flour, baking powder, salt, and xanthan gum in mixing bowl. Make a well in the center and stir in ricotta cheese, eggs, sugar, candied fruit, raisins, almonds, and lemon peel. Knead lightly until the dough holds together.

Shape into one 12-inch-long loaf and place on a greased and rice-floured cookie sheet. Bake 50 to 60 minutes in preheated 375° oven, or until a toothpick inserted in the center comes out clean. Transfer to wire rack.

Brush melted butter over the warm loaf; sift powdered sugar over the top. Cool completely. Slice to serve.

ORANGE CORNBREAD
STUFFING

Roast turkey with sausage and orange cornbread dressing was a traditional Thanksgiving favorite in the Old South. It's excellent, too, for those on a gluten-free diet. But don't save it just for Thanksgiving. Use it with Cornish game hens, roast chicken, or pork (eliminating the sausage).

1 recipe Orange Cornbread, page 46	1/2 cup sliced celery
	2 eggs, beaten
Optional: 1/2 pound bulk pork sausage	1 teaspoon dried thyme
	1/2 teaspoon salt
1 medium onion, diced	1 to 1 1/2 cups chicken stock
Optional: 1/2 cup green pepper, chopped	

Prepare orange cornbread, using only 2 eggs. Cool, crumble, and set aside.

In a large skillet, sauté the sausage, onion, green pepper, and celery until meat is browned and vegetables just tender. Drain thoroughly.

In mixing bowl, combine the sausage mixture, eggs, thyme, and salt. Add the crumbled cornbread and toss until well mixed. Add enough stock to moisten to desired consistency. The full amount of stock will make a moist dressing. If you prefer it drier, cut the amount of liquid.

Makes enough to stuff a 12- to 14-pound bird. Or you may bake it in a greased 2¹/₂-quart casserole in preheated 325° oven for about 45 minutes.

RICE BREAD STUFFING

If you don't want to make the cornbread recipe, you can use up your stale rice bread or use those crumbs salvaged from bread recipes that failed and still have a stuffing everyone will praise.

1 large onion, minced	2 tablespoons minced parsley
1 cup diced celery	6 to 8 cups GF bread, crumbled
6 tablespoons (³/₄ stick) butter or margarine	1 to 1¹/₂ cups chicken broth
1 to 1¹/₂ teaspoons poultry seasoning	Salt to taste

Sauté the onion and celery in butter until clear; add the poultry seasoning and parsley. Pour this mixture over the bread in a large mixing bowl. Stir until blended, then add the broth, a little at a time, until the dressing is as moist as you prefer. Add salt to taste. *Makes enough to stuff a 10- to 12-pound turkey.*

SEASONED BREAD: If you are baking your GF bread near the holiday season, try putting the 1 to 1¹/₂ teaspoons poultry seasoning directly into the dough for at least one loaf before you bake it. Try adding some dried minced parsley, also. This seasoned bread will make excellent stuffing and win you raves. It works best with the True Yeast Bread recipe (page 25), using white rice flour.

DESSERTS

PRESIDENTS' DAY
CHERRY CHEESE PIE

It's hard to believe something so good could be so easy. A fine dessert for the holiday.

One 8-ounce package
  cream cheese
One 14-ounce can
  sweetened condensed
  milk
1/3 cup lemon juice

1 teaspoon vanilla
1 Cereal Crust, page 91,
  or Crumb Crust,
  page 91
One 21-ounce can GF
  cherry pie filling

In a mixing bowl, soften the cream cheese, then beat until fluffy. Beat in the sweetened condensed milk until smooth. Stir in the lemon juice and vanilla. Pour into the prepared crust. Chill 3 hours or until set. Top with pie filling. Keep pie refrigerated. *Makes 6 to 8 servings.*

MOCK MINCE PIE

A light substitute for old-fashioned mincemeat pie. My tasters all agreed it was excellent.

1 recipe Tender Vinegar
Pastry, page 90
1 1/3 cups sugar
1/2 teaspoon salt
1/2 teaspoon cinnamon
1/4 teaspoon cloves
1/4 teaspoon ginger
2 cups peeled, chopped
apple
1 cup raisins
One 8-ounce can cranberry
sauce

1/3 cup chopped walnuts
or pecans
1 teaspoon dried orange
peel
1 teaspoon dried lemon
peel
3 tablespoons lemon juice
1 tablespoon milk for
brushing
1/2 teaspoon sugar for
brushing

Prepare pastry and fit bottom crust into a deep 9″ pie pan.

Place all remaining ingredients in a large mixing bowl and toss together lightly. Place in the pie crust. Top with the second crust. Cut vents. Brush the top with 1 tablespoon milk and 1/2 teaspoon sugar and bake at 400° in preheated oven for 30 to 35 minutes. Serve warm, but the wedges keep their shape better if this is made ahead, cooled, and then cut into servings and reheated. *Makes 6 servings.*

OLD-FASHIONED PUMPKIN PIE

We've put pumpkin in breads, mousses, and fluffed it into chiffon pies, but most true pumpkin pie lovers still ask for old-fashioned pie for their Thanksgiving dessert.

2 eggs
One 16-ounce can
pumpkin
3/4 cup sugar
1/2 teaspoon salt

2 teaspoons pumpkin pie
spice
1 1/2 cups cream or
nondairy substitute
1 Cereal Crust, page 91

In a large mixing bowl, beat the eggs slightly. Add pumpkin, sugar, salt, and spice. Stir together. Add the cream and mix thoroughly. Pour into the unbaked crust. Bake in preheated 425° oven for 15 minutes. Reduce temperature to 350° and bake another 45 minutes, or until knife inserted in the center of the pie comes out clean. Cool.

Serve cold with whipped cream or whipped nondairy topping if desired. *Makes 6 to 8 servings.*

TROPICAL FRUITCAKE

This rich, moist fruitcake is pure fruit and nuts. Once you've tasted it, you won't seek another recipe. But be forewarned, it is addictive.

2 1/4 cups pecans	One 14-ounce can
1 3/4 cups walnuts	sweetened condensed
1 pound pitted dates	milk
8 ounces candied	4 ounces shredded
cherries	coconut, or substitute
8 ounces candied pineapple	macadamia nuts

Chop the pecans, walnuts, and dates. Cut up the cherries and pineapple. Slice the macadamia nuts (if used).

Combine pecans, walnuts, dates, cherries, pineapple, condensed milk, and coconut or macadamia nuts. Mix with hands.

Pack tightly into three greased and rice-floured small (3″ × 6″) baking tins. Bake in preheated 250° oven for about 3 hours. Cake is done when no milk oozes out when pressed with fingers.

Cool in pans turned on their side. Remove to foil and wrap snugly. Store in refrigerator or freezer about 1 month before serving.

If you prefer, you may use 1 large 5″ × 8″ × 4″ loaf pan, but this is a rich cake and pieces should be cut small for serving.

CHRISTMAS FRUITCAKE

This excellent fruitcake is more spicy and cakelike than the preceding one. It also stores and freezes well. The taste will vary according to the mincemeat used and the types of fruit and nuts. Try pecans for variety.

2 eggs
28 ounces (2²/₃ cups)
   mincemeat*
One 14-ounce can
   sweetened condensed
   milk
16 ounces candied fruits

1 cup chopped walnuts
2 cups rice flour
¹/₂ cup soy flour
1 teaspoon salt
2¹/₂ teaspoons baking
   powder
1 teaspoon baking soda

In a large mixing bowl, beat the eggs slightly, add mincemeat, condensed milk, candied fruits, and nuts. Then mix together the flours, salt, baking powder, and baking soda. Fold the dry mixture into the fruit mixture.

Pour into greased and rice-floured pans. Use either a 12-cup ring baking pan or 2 large loaf pans. Bake 2 hours in preheated 300° to 325° oven.

When done, cool in pan. Remove and store in refrigerator or freezer.

*Check ingredient list. (Some mincemeats contain wheat starch flour, others cornstarch.) I have used the dried mincemeat that you reconstitute with water, and find it works well.

MOTHER'S PLUM PUDDING

Plum pudding was a Christmas tradition in our house. This recipe, handed down from my mother's English family, made an instant hit with everyone when I converted it to rice and soy flours. My guests now ask for this rather than the original recipe. It is inexpensive, light, and moist. Like all plum puddings, it can be made several days ahead, thus saving the cook's time for enjoying Christmas. (Remember to save your 19-ounce cans in the weeks before embarking on this recipe.)

3/4 cup rice flour	1 1/2 cups brown sugar
3/4 cup soy flour	1 cup raisins
1 rounded teaspoon baking soda	1 1/2 cups chopped raw cranberries
1/2 teaspoon salt	1 cup ground suet
1 teaspoon each cinnamon, nutmeg, cloves	1 cup ground raw carrots
	1 cup ground raw potatoes

Sift together flours, baking soda, salt, and spices. Blend in brown sugar. Stir in fruit, suet, carrots, and potatoes.

Grease 3 cans of approximately 19 ounces each. (Or use a 2-quart can for mold.) Fill cans three-quarters full. Seal tops with wax paper and then aluminum foil. Keep airtight with rubber bands. Put molds in a deep dutch oven or soup pot in enough water to maintain steam around them for 3 hours of cooking on top of the stove. These should be covered, and no peeking except to check water. Be sure it doesn't boil away. You should be able to maintain steam by setting most stoves at simmer or low.

Store puddings in refrigerator after cooling. They keep well for a week or more, or, if made earlier, can be frozen. Serve, reheated, with whipped cream or hard sauce.

NOTE: The original recipe used tart apples, but when cranberries became a popular holiday item, my mother switched to them. You may use apples if you prefer.

THE GLUTEN-FREE DIET

A diet free of the cereal protein gluten found in all grains except corn and rice (no wheat, oats, rye, or barley).

Foods Allowed	Foods to Avoid

BEVERAGES

Foods Allowed	Foods to Avoid
Coffee, tea, carbonated beverages, cocoa (Baker's, Hershey's, Nestlé), rum, tequila, vodka (if made from potatoes or grapes), wine (if not fortified with grain alcohol as found in some imported wines).	Postum, Ovaltine, beer, ale, gin, vodka (if made from grain), wine (if fortified with grain alcohol), whiskey (bourbon, scotch, and rye), some flavored coffees, some herbal teas.

BREADS

Foods Allowed	Foods to Avoid
Breads made with gluten-free flours only (rice, potato starch, soy, tapioca, corn), either baked at home or purchased from companies that produce GF products. Rice crackers, corn tortillas.	All breads made with wheat, oats, rye, barley flours. All purchased crackers, croutons, bread crumbs, wafers, biscuits, and doughnuts containing any gluten flours. Graham, soda or snack crackers, tortillas containing wheat.

Foods Allowed	Foods to Avoid

CEREALS

Cornmeal, Cream of Rice, hominy grits, gluten-free cold rice and corn cereals (those without malt).	All cereals containing wheat, rye, oat, or barley (both grain and in flavoring, such as malt flavoring, malt syrup).

DAIRY PRODUCTS

Milk (fresh, dry, evaporated, or condensed), buttermilk, cream, sour cream, butter, cheese (except those that contain oat gum), whipped cream, yogurt (plain or flavored, if GF), ice cream (if GF), artificial cream (if GF).	Malted milk, artificial cream (if not GF), some chocolate milk drinks, some commercial ice creams, some processed cheese spreads, flavored yogurt (containing gluten).

DESSERTS

Any pie, cake, cookie, and so on made with GF flours and flavorings, gelatins, custards, homemade puddings (rice, cornstarch, tapioca).	All pies, cakes, cookies, and so on that contain any wheat, oat, rye, or barley flour or flavoring, most commercial pudding mixes, ice cream cones, prepared cake mixes.

FATS

Margarine, butter, vegetable oil, nuts, GF mayonnaise, shortening, lard, some salad dressings.	Some commercial salad dressings, some mayonnaise.

FLOURS

Rice flour (brown and white), soy flour, potato starch flour, potato flour, tapioca flour, corn flour, cornmeal, cornstarch, rice bran, rice polish.	All flours containing wheat, rye, oats, and/or barley. Semolina.

Foods Allowed	Foods to Avoid

FRUITS AND JUICES

All fruit, fresh, frozen, canned (if GF), and dried.	Any commercially canned fruit with gluten thickening.

MEAT, FISH, POULTRY, AND EGGS

Any eggs (plain or in cooking), all fresh meats, fish, poultry, other seafood, fish canned in oil or brine, GF prepared meats such as hot dogs, luncheon meats.	Eggs in gluten-based sauce, seafood that contains gluten-based sirimi, prepared meats that contain gluten (like some luncheon meats and hot dogs), some fish canned in vegetable broth, self-basting turkeys injected with hydrolyzed vegetable protein (HVP).

PASTAS

GF homemade noodles, spaghetti, macaroni, and so on. Oriental rice noodles, bean threads. Some GF brands of pasta made with corn, tapioca, and potato flours.	Regular noodles, spaghetti, macaroni, and so on. Any canned pasta product.

SOUPS AND CHOWDERS

Homemade broth and soups made with GF ingredients, some canned soups, some powdered soup bases, some GF dehydrated soups.	Most canned soups, most dehydrated soup mixes, bouillon and bouillon cubes containing hydrolyzed vegetable protein (HVP).

SWEETS

Jellies, jams, honey, sugar, molasses, corn syrup, syrup, some commercial candies.	Some commercial candy, Marshmallow Creme, cake decorations, marzipan.

Foods Allowed	Foods to Avoid

VEGETABLES

All plain fresh, frozen, or canned vegetables, dried peas, beans, and lentils.	All creamed, breaded, and escalloped vegetables. Some canned baked beans, some prepared salad mixes.

CONDIMENTS

Salt, pepper, herbs, food coloring, pure spices, vinegar (except grain distilled), yeast, GF soy sauce, GF curry powder, baking powder, baking soda, MSG if made in USA.	Some curry powder, some mixed spices, grain-distilled vinegar, some catsup, some prepared mustards, most soy sauces.

This list was compiled from information supplied to the author by her physician, the Gluten Intolerance Group of North America, and the Cleveland Clinic Foundation.

It is just a general list for your information. Always remember to read the full ingredient list when purchasing any product that might contain any form of gluten. If in doubt, write to the manufacturer about ingredients used in packaging or processing.

WHERE TO FIND
GLUTEN-FREE PRODUCTS

Cooking gluten free is going to take more shopping at first than for ordinary cooking, but once the sources have been found for these flours, flavorings, and the additives (like xanthan gum), you will probably find it consumes no more of your time than it did before.

Some of the flours and flavorings can be found in supermarkets, some in health food or specialty stores, and the rest can be ordered by mail. Often, with just one free long-distance phone call, you can have your gluten-free baking supplies on their way to arrive in less than a week.

The following companies accept orders by mail or phone or both:

The Allergy Shop (GF pastas, flour, baking mixes, baking supplies, baked bread, cakes, cookies and pastries, books), #10, 630 - 1 Avenue N.E., Calgary, Alberta T2E OB6; phone (403) 262-8608, fax (403) 279-4105.

Alpineaire Foods (freeze-dried foods for camping with complete ingredient list available), PO Box 926, Nevada City, CA 95959; phone (916) 272-1971. Write or call for a free catalog. Some products can be found in specialty sporting goods stores.

Arrowhead Mills, Inc. (GF flours, rice, beans, cereals, and pancake mixes), PO Box 2059, Hereford, TX 79045; phone (806) 364-0730. Some products may be found in health food and gourmet stores.

Bickford Flavors (gluten-free flavorings), 19007 St. Clair Avenue, Cleveland, OH 44117-1001; phone (800) 283-8322. Products can also be found in health food and specialty food stores.

Celia Cooks (gluten-free condiments, convenience foods, snacks, and desserts), PO Box 728, Ramsey, NJ 07446; phone (201) 934-0987. Accepts orders only by mail, but phone for the latest catalog and price list.

Cybros, Inc. (rice bread, rolls, and nuggets, gluten-free cookies), PO Box 851, Waukesha, WI 53187-0851; phone (800) 876-2253. Their products can also be found in health food stores.

Dietary Specialties, Inc. (xanthan and guar gum, Drei Pauly and rice pasta, cookies, crackers, mixes for breads, cakes, etc., cereal and flavorings, gluten-free cookbooks), PO Box 227, Rochester, NY 14601; phone (800) 544-0099. Write or phone for their complete list.

Elles Gluten-Free (formerly Sterk's Bakery, Ltd.) (guar gum, gluten-free flours, baked breads, rolls, cakes, pizza crust; baking mixes, etc.), 3866 23d Street, Vineland, Ontario, Canada L0R 2C0 or M.P.O. Box 2703, Niagara Falls, NY 14302; phone (416) 562-3086. Write for list of products made with guar gum.

El Peto Products (bean, rice and other GF flours, pasta, breads, soups, sauces and snack foods, cookbooks), 41 Shoemaker Street Unit 2, Kitchener, Ontario N2E 3G9; phone (510) 748-5211. Phone or write for their list.

Ener-G-Foods, Inc. (xanthan and guar gum, gluten-free flours, GF Gourmet flour mix, Egg Replacer, Lacto-Free, baked bread, cookies, pizza shells, and other baked products, mixes, cereals, pasta, soup mixes, gluten-free cookbooks, etc.), PO Box 84487, Seattle, WA 98124-5787; phone (800) 331-5222; in Wash. state (800) 325-9788. Phone for a catalog of their long list. Ener-G-Foods products can also be found in some health food stores and specialty markets.

Foodcare, Inc. (food allergy specialists; GF flours, cereals, pasta, candies), PO Box 40, 205 South Main, Seymour, IL 61875; phone (217) 687-5115. Ask for their catalog and fact/recipe sheets.

Food for Life Baking Co., Inc. (gluten-free breads, muffins, pasta), 2991 East Doherty Street, Corona, CA 91719; phone (714) 279-5090. Their products may also be found in natural food stores and some groceries under the Food for Life label.

The Gluten-Free Pantry (gourmet baking mixes for pancakes, bread, and cookies), PO Box 881, Glastonbury, CT 06033; phone (203) 633-3826.

King Arthur Flour (tapioca flour, white rice flour, potato starch flour, xanthan gum), PO Box 876, Norwich, VT 05055; phone (800) 827-6836. Request King Arthur Flour Baker's Catalog.

Kinnikinnick Foods (GF baking supplies and flours, prepared mixes, pastas, cereals, cookies, etc.), 9857 76 Avenue, Edmonton, Alberta T6E 1K6; phone (403) 433-4023. Phone or write for their list.

Legumes Plus, Inc. (gluten-free baking mix; lentil soup, chili, casserole and salad mixes; snack bar), PO Box 383, Fairfield, WA 99012; phone (800) 845-1349. Some products can also be found in health and gourmet food stores and specialty supermarkets.

Life Force Nutritional Products, Inc. (spice blends for ethnic dishes, gluten free, low sodium), PO Box 1317, San Marcos, CA 92069-1317; phone (818) 952-4433. Phone or write for their list of Spices for Life Bouquet Line. Mail order only.

Life Source Natural Food Limited (rice pasta, spinach rice pasta, tomato rice pasta), 91 Esna Park Drive, Markham, Ontario, Canada L3R 2S2; United States phone (416) 475-6836. Sold through health food stores. Call to inquire where distributed in your area.

Lundberg Family Farms (brown rice and rice blends, aromatic rice blends, Riz Cous, rice cakes, hot rice cereal), PO Box 369, Richvale, CA 95974-0369; phone (916) 882-4551. Write for their order form. These products may also be found in health food stores and grocery stores with natural food sections.

Mallard Pond Farms (popcorn flour), 746 Mallard Pond Drive, Boulder, CO 80303; phone (800) 533-2676; in Denver area, 494-3551.

Moore Natural Foods (xanthan and guar gum, gluten-free flours, cereals and rice, pastas, legumes, soup mixes, yeast, gluten-free cookbooks), 5209 S.E. International Way, Milwaukie, OR 97222; phone (503) 654-3215. Call or write for their order form. Some of their products can be found under Bob's Red Mill label in health food stores and in health sections of regular grocery stores.

Pamela's Products, Inc. (gluten-free flours, breads, cookies, baking mixes), 136 Utah Avenue, South San Francisco, CA 94080; phone (415) 952-4546. Some products may also be found in health food stores under the Delightful Alternatives label.

The Really Great Food Co. (GF baking mixes for corn bread, pancakes, muffins, pizza crust; cereals, rice flour mix), PO Box 319, Malverne, NY 11565; phone (516) 593-5587. Call or write for their product list.

Red Mill Farms, Inc. (gluten-free cakes and macaroons), Gluten-free Products Division, 290 South 5th Street, Brooklyn, NY 11211; phone (718) 384-2150. Mail-order only. Write for their product list. Also sold in health food stores as Jennies of Red Mill Farms.

Miss Roben's (xanthan and guar gum, gluten-free baking mixes), PO Box 1434, Frederick, MD 21702; phone (800) 891-0083. Some products can be found in local health food stores.

Specialty Food Shop (bread, cookies, baking mixes, granola bar called muesli cookie, dry pasta, canned pasta, fruit cake), Radio Centre Plaza, Lower Level Mall, 875 Main Street West, Hamilton, Ontario, Canada L8S 4P9; phone: Canada, (800) 268-7010; United States, (416) 528-4707. Write for their list of gluten-free products sold under the Kingsmill or Rite Diet labels.

Tad Enterprises (xanthan gum, gluten-free flours, bread mix, baked products, cereals, pasta), 9356 Pleasant, Tinley Park, IL 60477; phone (708) 429-2101. Write for their order form and complete list of products offered.

This list was updated at the time of publication of this book. The author regrets she cannot be responsible for later changes in the above information.

INDEX

Green split peas. *See* Split peas, green
    or yellow
Guacamole Dip, 125
Guar gum, notes on, 13–14

Ham
    and Cheese Quiche, 174
    and Chicken Pasta, 153–54
    in Hillbilly Soup, 146
    hock, in Split Pea Soup, 144–45
    in Monte Cristo Sandwich, 172
    as pizza topping, 164
    Scalloped Potatoes and, 178
    in Vegetable Quiche with Mashed
      Potato Crust, 114–15
Hamburger
    Buns, 26
    patties, as gluten danger, 8–9
Hash browns, as gluten danger, 8–9
Hawaiian Curry, 183–84
Hawaiian Delight Meringues, 192–93
Hawaiian Tea Bread, 36
Hearty Chicken Noodle Soup, 141
Hello Dollys, 56
Hillbilly Soup (16-Bean Soup), 146
Homemade Chili, 182
Homemade Pasta, 150–51
Hot Cross Buns, 208–9
Hot Curried Fruit, 202
Hot dogs, gluten-free, in Pups in Blan-
    kets, 122
Huckleberries, for blackberries in
    Blackberry Dumplings, 199
Hydrolyzed vegetable protein (HVP),
    gluten in, 6

Icing. *See also* Frosting
    Chocolate, Easy, 85
Infant formula, for milk in recipes, x
Instant or powdered coffee, as gluten
    danger, 8

Jam
    Cake, Country, 77–78
    -Filled Crunchies, 61–62

Jill's Quick and Easy Pizza Crust,
    161
Julekaka, 33

Kasha (Buckwheat) Muffins, 41–42
Kidney beans
    in Calico Beans, 183
    red, in Hillbilly Soup, 146
Kielbasa sausage, in Sausage and Len-
    til Bake, 179–80

Lasagne
    Three-Cheese, 155
    Vegetarian, 155–56
Latkes (Potato Pancakes), 207–8
Leek, Potato, Soup, 137–38
Lemon
    Lemon Pie, 95
    Sheet Cake, 68
    Sponge Pie, 99–100
Lentil(s)
    in Hillbilly Soup, 146
    Sausage and, Bake, 179–80
    Sesame Bread, 38–39
    Soup, 145
Lima beans
    in Calico Beans, 183
    in Hillbilly Soup, 146
Lime Sponge Pudding, 198–99
Linda's Lighter Cheesecake, 81
Loganberries
    in Berry Cobbler, 196
    for blackberries, in Blackberry
      Dumplings, 199
    in Deep-dish Berry Pie with a Cream
      Cheese Crust, 194

Macaroons, Coconut, 52
Mandarin oranges, in Wine Curried
    Fruit, 203
Maraschino cherries, in Wine Curried
    Fruit, 203
Mashed Potato Crust, Vegetable
    Quiche with, 114–15
Mayonnaise Chicken Casserole, 176